Start Investing in Alternative Assets

Start Investing in Alternative Assets

Explore whiskey, royalties, collectibles, farmland, and more unique opportunities

Julian Thorne

Mindful Pages

Published in 2025

ISBN: 9789371776899 (PB)
ISBN: 9789371774345 (eBook)

Published by

Mindful Pages
Imprint of Alpha Editions LLC
312 W. 2nd St #1834
Casper, WY 82601, USA

This book was developed using advanced writing tools to support the drafting and ideation process. All content has been thoughtfully curated, refined, and reviewed to ensure quality and relevance.

Content

Introduction
A New Map of Value

The conception of wealth is quietly shifting. Slowly, almost imperceptibly, the old coordinates that once guided investors—the rigid binaries of risk and reward, the sanctity of traditional asset classes, the comfort of standardised diversification metrics—are being reconsidered, redrawn, and in some instances, abandoned. For decades, personal finance offered a linear script: accumulate savings, spread investments across stocks and bonds, endure market cycles, and retire into safety. Predictable, methodical, reassuring. Yet in today's economic and cultural climate, that framework feels constrained, occasionally out of sync with the complexity of modern financial life.

Start Investing in Alternative Assets begins with a provocation: what if the most valuable holdings are those that conventional finance struggles to quantify? What if returns alone no longer define significance? This is not a critique of performance—it remains crucial—but a challenge to the notion that performance alone encapsulates value. In a world shaped by technological acceleration, cultural volatility, and existential uncertainty, spreadsheets and pie charts are no longer sufficient. We require a map of value attuned to human resonance as much as monetary yield.

Investing has always been about more than money. Identity, aspiration, permanence, belief—these are inseparable from the act of ownership. Whether a pre-war Burgundy, a first-edition book, a hardwood grove in Oregon, or the royalties from a globally recognised song, alternative assets are more than profit vehicles; they are expressions of taste, worldview, and temporal judgment. They demand attention calibrated to nuance, reward discernment, and invite reflection: what, truly, is worth owning?

The boundaries between finance and culture are dissolving. Football clubs become instruments of cultural influence rather than mere revenue streams. Hedge funds acquire music catalogues as much for prestige as profit. Young investors pursue whiskey barrels and collectible cards with the seriousness prior generations reserved for index funds. These shifts signal more than fleeting trends; they reveal a broader evolution in what society values.

This book is not a catalogue of curiosities, nor a checklist of alternative assets. It is a philosophical and practical guide to capital deployment that accounts for story, scarcity, and curiosity. Here, speculation is never disguised as certainty, nor hype as insight. Instead, the reader is invited to perceive the world more sharply, to approach a portfolio with both discernment and imagination.

At its core, this exploration speaks to a new breed of investor: one who prizes meaning alongside metrics. Perhaps passive vehicles no longer satisfy; perhaps conventional diversification feels illusory in a market where correlation spikes under stress. Or perhaps the appeal is simply aesthetic—a wealth that is textured, personal, and alive.

We begin with desire itself. Alternative assets operate in the realm of emotion. Behavioural finance has illuminated the cognitive biases shaping decisions, yet seldom do we interrogate why certain objects captivate us. Why the rare, the storied, the original? Not purely for economic reward; the answers lie in identity signalling, cultural narratives, and the brain's reward systems.

From desire, we move to structure. True diversification is often illusory: portfolios that appear varied may move in lockstep under stress. Genuine non-correlation increasingly exists outside mainstream markets—in farmland, film rights, or fine art. Engaging these requires a lens that prizes longevity over liquidity.

Subsequent chapters navigate both specificity and breadth. The whiskey market, where time and temperature create not only flavour but value. Intellectual property, where royalties become contemporary dividends. Vintage watches, where design, durability, and memory intertwine to generate financial and cultural capital. Wine and art further illustrate taste-driven investing, demonstrating how connoisseurship itself cultivates market literacy. Land—arable soil, managed forests—reminds us that physical ownership confers power, permanence, and continuity.

Digital assets cannot be ignored. NFTs, virtual real estate, Web3 tokens: scarcity encoded on chains yet still mediated by human judgement. We evaluate these with scepticism tempered by openness, examining what confers value and what is merely ephemeral.

Where novelty exists, so too does risk. Not every whiskey barrel appreciates; not every song will sustain royalties; not every digital collectible retains worth. A dedicated chapter addresses fraud, hype, and the red flags endemic to emerging markets. This is a book for the curious and grounded, not the dazzled or impulsive.

Ultimately, the work asks: what do your investments reveal about you? Beyond abstraction, a portfolio is a personal museum—a curated assemblage of values, aspirations, and beliefs. Some assets are bought to sell, others to hold, a rare few to embody one's identity. Here, investing becomes art. Ownership blends utility and symbolism. A bottle of whiskey becomes a time capsule; farmland, a wager on continuity. Ownership carries responsibility alongside rights.

Wealth, when meaningful, transcends the financial.

Start Investing in Alternative Assets does not prescribe what to buy. It equips readers to think differently, to approach markets with rigour and imagination. It advocates sophistication, not speculation; stewardship, not status; intention over default.

The terrain ahead is unconventional, the path unfamiliar. Yet for those who sense that opportunity often lies off the beaten track, this journey is precisely where to begin.

Welcome. Let us proceed.

Chapter 1
The Psychology of Desire and Rarity

What drives a collector to spend six figures on a bottle of whiskey destined never to be opened? Why will an investor queue for years to secure a rare watch when more precise, more durable alternatives exist at a fraction of the cost? And why do some of the world's most sophisticated portfolios contain holdings that seem—at first glance—utterly irrational by conventional financial logic? The answer lies not in balance sheets or asset allocation algorithms, but in subtler forces: emotion, narrative, identity, and the magnetic appeal of rarity.

To grasp alternative assets, one must first confront the human heart behind the decision.

For decades, investing literature has valorised objectivity—rational choices, calibrated risk, emotional detachment. Money was to be treated as abstract, a tool governed by formulas. Yet in practice, investors are far from abstract. They are social beings, shaped by personal history, cultural scripts, and psychological wiring. What they purchase, covet, or hold reflects not only market signals but aspirations, identity markers, and symbolic resonance.

This chapter proposes a recalibration. The lens shifts from assets themselves to the appetites they awaken. Objects—the whiskey cask, the first-edition novel, the vintage watch—derive much of their value from extrinsic associations. Rarity, provenance, narrative: these are the levers that animate price and demand. They are psychological as much as financial.

Behavioural finance has illuminated biases like anchoring, loss aversion, and overconfidence, yet underlying these patterns is something more elemental: desire. Desire is not an aberration; it is a guiding principle. The longing for uniqueness, the thrill of distinction, the satisfaction of owning what others cannot—these impulses are not anomalies. They are central to alternative investing.

Neuroeconomics underscores this reality. Exposure to scarce or culturally potent objects—be it a limited-edition vinyl or a luxury timepiece—activates dopamine pathways, rewarding more than utility alone. Social signalling, personal gratification, and perceived prestige converge. In these moments, the investor acts less as a rational optimiser than as an emotionally engaged participant in a theatre of scarcity and meaning.

Narrative power explains why certain alternative assets outperform expectations. A watch owned by a cultural icon, a vineyard with centuries of lineage, a music catalogue that defined an era—economic value is inseparable from the story attached. And stories are contagious: they circulate among collectors, investors, and connoisseurs, reinforcing cultural cachet and enhancing perceived value.

Consider rare books. A first edition of *The Great Gatsby* commands hundreds of thousands of pounds—not for textual difference, but for its aura. The object is a tangible relic, a status symbol, a touchstone of history. Across categories, the principle holds: whiskey, art, or timepieces are purchased as much for story, prestige, and symbolic capital as for their material properties.

Symbolic capital is central to understanding alternative investments. Unlike equities, often invisible outside financial statements, many alternative assets are performative. They signal taste, identity, and belonging. Owning a Banksy communicates cultural literacy. Investing in bourbon barrels evokes heritage, craftsmanship, and subtle rebellion. A portfolio, in this sense, becomes biography: curated, expressive, and socially legible.

Social signalling is strategic, not superficial. Elite investors prize assets that are difficult to acquire or comprehend precisely because they confer status through obscurity and expertise. Stocks are available to anyone. Navigating vintage watches or rare wines demands networks, refined judgment, and cultural fluency. The barrier to entry amplifies allure: ownership is earned, not merely purchased.

Yet rarity alone does not guarantee value. Not all stories appreciate. The market rewards resonance—assets that harmonise personal meaning with collective recognition. Paul Newman's Rolex, for instance, is prized not for mechanics but for the cultural narrative it embodies. Story is intrinsic to the asset's economic value.

We might call this the "story premium," a concept increasingly salient in an era of information overload and fleeting attention. A sherry-cask-aged whiskey carries narrative richness that mass-produced spirits lack, even when composition is comparable. Perception, informed by story, drives demand. Scarcity matters, but narrative transforms scarcity into significance.

This principle extends beyond luxury or cultural artefacts. Farmland, timber, and other utilitarian assets accrue symbolic meaning over time—legacy, stewardship, or a hedge against existential uncertainty. The transition from functional to symbolic alters pricing, ownership, and stewardship. Investors become custodians, not merely allocators.

Across markets, the pattern repeats. A wristwatch becomes heritage; soil becomes statement; royalties become cultural participation. Purchases are no longer simply output—they are lenses through which to interpret value, time, and identity.

Financial fundamentals remain essential: market dynamics, liquidity, and legal frameworks cannot be ignored. Yet in alternative assets, emotional, social, and symbolic factors are not peripheral—they define the terrain. Successful engagement demands interdisciplinary fluency: psychology, sociology, history, and aesthetics are as vital as balance sheets. Decoding meaning, anticipating trends, and appreciating emotional resonance become competitive edges.

The chapters ahead examine how desire, scarcity, and story drive value: from neurological impulses behind ownership to the social mechanics of collectability, from myth-making to strategic signalling. Rational analysis remains necessary, but it is enriched—and sometimes eclipsed—by narrative. Numbers matter. Story matters. Increasingly, the two are inseparable.

Understanding the psychology of desire and rarity is crucial not only for navigating alternative assets but for comprehending the evolving nature of capital itself. As money, meaning, and identity converge, the investor of the future will need a fluency that speaks both the language of finance and the dialects of culture.

That fluency begins here.

The Emotional Blueprint of Ownership

There is a peculiar intensity that grips people in the moment of acquiring something rare. It might be a vintage wristwatch, the rights to a timeless song, or a centuries-old bottle of wine. Often, the acquisition is less about the object itself than what it represents—an idea, a memory, a version of self. To the casual observer, the value might seem abstract or inflated. To the investor, however, it feels self-evident, even essential. What's occurring in that moment is not merely a transaction—it's a neurological and psychological event, one that defies the purely rational models on which so much of classical finance has been built.

Traditional economics assumes that investors behave like calculators: logical, detached, guided by probabilities and outcomes. But real investors—human investors—are deeply emotional creatures. Their decisions are shaped by memory, identity, and social comparison just as much as they are by expected returns. In the world of alternative assets, where tangibility, symbolism, and narrative carry disproportionate weight, emotional drivers become even more potent. And rather than being flaws in the system, these emotional forces are the very blueprint through which value is perceived, pursued, and ultimately, possessed.

At the centre of this dynamic is desire. Desire is not a passing mood; it is a structured, biologically anchored drive. Neuroscience has shown that the pursuit of something novel or scarce activates the brain's dopaminergic pathways—the same circuits responsible for motivation, anticipation, and pleasure. Crucially, dopamine is not released upon receiving a reward, but in anticipation of it. The thrill of the chase, the scarcity of the object, the imagined status of ownership—all of these conspire to make the pre-acquisition phase neurologically charged. For investors in alternative assets, this anticipation can become as rewarding as the asset itself.

This helps explain why auctions, exclusivity, and limited releases are so effective. These aren't merely marketing strategies; they're psychological triggers. When a bottle of whisky is one of only fifty ever released, or a digital artwork is minted with a verifiable single-owner provenance, the rarity cues set off a complex emotional calculus. Scarcity doesn't just imply limited supply—it signals that the item is worthy of being limited, worthy of attention, and by extension, worthy of desire. In that moment, owning the item becomes a proxy for distinction.

But this emotional blueprint is not driven by dopamine alone. Identity plays a central role. What we choose to own reflects who we believe ourselves to be—or who we aspire to become. A collector of first-edition novels might see himself not merely as an investor, but as a custodian of literary history. A buyer of regenerative farmland may be expressing values around sustainability, legacy, and permanence. In these cases, ownership becomes autobiographical. The portfolio is no longer just a financial statement; it's a curated expression of self.

This identity alignment becomes even more significant when considering the social dimensions of investment. Ownership of rare or storied assets functions as a kind of coded language—signalling taste, education, and insider status to those who can decode it. Unlike traditional assets, which are often invisible and generic, many alternative assets are conspicuous by design. A rare watch, a blue-chip painting, a rare bottle of Burgundy—these are objects that live in the open, interpreted and admired by those within the know. And that interpretation reinforces value.

Social psychology has long studied the phenomenon of conspicuous consumption—buying to signal status. But in the upper tiers of alternative investing, what's being signalled is more nuanced than mere wealth. It is discernment. Cultural capital. Depth. To own the right piece of contemporary art is to signal one's fluency in the language of aesthetic relevance. To hold rights to a catalogue of jazz classics is to affiliate oneself with a lineage of artistry and authenticity. These signals are not accidental by-products; they are part of the value proposition.

There is a common misconception that such motivations dilute the seriousness of investing. That to be swayed by aesthetics, symbolism, or emotion is to deviate from financial rigour. But this view is outdated. In a marketplace where perception shapes demand and demand shapes price, emotional resonance *is* a form of value. Indeed, some of the world's most successful collectors and investors are those who intuitively understand how emotion scales—how personal meaning can metastasise into public desirability, and thus into economic return.

Consider the example of vintage watches. A Rolex Submariner produced in the 1960s might cost ten times as much as its modern counterpart, despite being technically inferior in precision and durability. What drives this discrepancy? Part of it is scarcity, but more of it is story. The Submariner isn't just a watch—it's a symbol, tied to cultural memory, craftsmanship heritage, and a kind of rugged elegance that lives more in imagination than on the wrist. Ownership, in this context, is an act of participation in that story.

The emotional blueprint of ownership also carries a temporal dimension. Alternative assets often require patience. They are not designed for immediate liquidity or algorithmic flipping. This delay between acquisition and outcome invites a different kind of investor psychology—one that values stewardship over speculation. And stewardship, by its nature, is an emotional commitment. To hold a cask of whisky for twenty years, to nurture a plot of vineyard, to maintain an artwork's condition through changing climates and curatorial fashions—these are all acts of care. They bind the investor not just to the asset, but to time itself.

There is also an ethical dimension to this emotional blueprint—one that deserves serious attention. When investment intersects with identity, the line between value creation and value extraction can blur. Is the collector preserving culture, or hoarding access? Is the farmland investor promoting sustainability, or displacing local ecosystems? These are not abstract questions. They define the stakes of ownership in the twenty-first century. As alternative assets become more mainstream, the emotional motivations that underlie investment decisions will increasingly shape outcomes beyond the portfolio—affecting communities, cultures, and even the environment.

Yet, despite its complexity, the emotional landscape of ownership is navigable. It can be understood, articulated, and even harnessed—if investors are willing to confront it honestly. This requires more than self-awareness; it requires fluency in the languages of psychology, culture, and aesthetics. It demands an investor who is not only financially literate, but emotionally intelligent—capable of interrogating not just *what* they want to own, but *why*.

Critically, not all emotional motivations are aligned with long-term value. Nostalgia can inflate prices beyond reason. Herd mentality can masquerade as discernment. And narrative appeal can obscure structural fragility. The emotionally intelligent investor must therefore balance engagement with scepticism—recognising the power of emotional drivers while remaining alert to their distortions. It is not a matter of eliminating emotion from investing, but of integrating it wisely.

The rise of alternative assets has brought this challenge into sharper focus. These markets do not operate on the pure logic of discounted cash flow. They thrive on perception, provenance, and emotional resonance. To succeed in them, one must abandon the fiction of the emotionless investor and instead embrace a more complex archetype: the thoughtful enthusiast, the strategic romantic, the curator of capital who knows that meaning moves markets.

To own something rare is not merely to possess it, but to participate in a larger narrative—personal, social, and historical. This is the essence of the emotional blueprint of ownership. And in the context of alternative investing, it is not peripheral. It is central. Understanding this blueprint is not just useful—it is indispensable to anyone who wishes to navigate these markets with clarity, purpose, and sophistication.

Scarcity, Status, and the Signal Effect

Scarcity is often misunderstood as a supply-side technicality—as if rarity alone explains why certain assets command extraordinary value. But scarcity, in the context of alternative investments, is never just about numbers. It's about meaning. It is socially constructed, emotionally potent, and strategically deployed. The economic value of a rare object is frequently less about its objective attributes and more about what it enables its owner to signal to others—taste, access, insight, legacy. In short, status. And in a world increasingly saturated by noise and sameness, status is not a trivial by-product of ownership. It is part of the architecture of value itself.

This is not a new idea. Thorstein Veblen, writing at the turn of the twentieth century, introduced the notion of conspicuous consumption—expenditures that exist primarily to display economic power. But Veblen's model assumed a relatively direct and materialist interpretation: wealth displayed for the sake of social elevation. What we see today in the markets for art, rare spirits, vintage watches, and other alternative assets is something more layered. Here, the signal effect is no longer simply about affluence. It is about cultural positioning. Sophistication. Curated expertise. A rare Bordeaux or a Banksy print doesn't just say "I can afford this." It says "I understand what this means."

That distinction is subtle but powerful. It transforms ownership into a form of communication, often coded, sometimes exclusive, and always relational. The asset becomes a proxy for a broader narrative—one that only those with sufficient cultural capital can fully interpret. A newcomer might see a minimalist canvas and scoff at its valuation. An insider sees a lineage, a movement, a moment in art history captured and invested in. The difference is knowledge, and knowledge is a form of capital just as valuable as liquidity.

Nowhere is this dynamic more apparent than in the art market. Art is perhaps the most socially contingent of all asset classes. Its value is not defined by yield or cash flow but by discourse—who is talking about it, collecting it, curating it. When a Basquiat painting sells for over £80 million, the sale is not merely about canvas and paint. It's a referendum on cultural relevance, a signal that the collector is aligned with a specific narrative of urban grit, racial politics, and artistic rebellion—all packaged in a format that is portable, displayable, and auctionable.

Consider the collector who acquires a Rothko. To the general public, the piece may look like blocks of colour. To the informed, it is a spiritual object, a philosophical gesture, a milestone in the evolution of abstraction. But it is also a flag. It signals participation in a club of aesthetes and financiers who traffic not just in commodities, but in interpretations. The collector is not merely buying art; they are buying interpretive power—the ability to see what others miss, to know what others don't, to belong where others can't.

The same applies in more tactile domains. Take the world of rare whisky. The Macallan 1926 Fine and Rare, a bottle that fetched over £1.5 million at auction, is not fundamentally about flavour. Most bottles from the same cask will never be opened. The value lies in its rarity, its provenance, and the cachet it confers on the owner. It functions as a statement piece—not necessarily displayed on a shelf, but often deployed in conversation, in curated collections, or as part of a narrative of cultivated wealth. The whisky, like the Rothko, is not merely an object; it is a social artefact.

This is the signal effect in action. And it plays out across every serious market for alternative assets. Rare watches, for instance, operate within tightly defined status hierarchies. A vintage Patek Philippe or early-model Rolex Daytona is not just a timekeeping device; it is a marker of patience, access, and appreciation for horological history. Because supply is limited and demand is filtered through networks of reputation and insider knowledge, the ability to acquire these items becomes a demonstration of one's social and cultural reach.

In each case, scarcity is only half the equation. The other half is recognition. A rare object that no one recognises as valuable may have sentimental or speculative worth, but it cannot function as a social signal. It must be legible to the right audience. This is what separates mere uniqueness from status-conferring rarity. For the signal to work, the object must exist within a shared cultural matrix where meaning is understood and appreciated. Without that, the item is just rare. With it, it becomes powerful.

This intersubjective nature of value—what philosophers call *shared intentionality*—is why certain assets appreciate exponentially. When enough people agree that a Damien Hirst spin painting or a closed-distillery Japanese whisky represents cultural significance, demand concentrates. And because supply is fixed or shrinking, the price reflects not only economic fundamentals but social heat. The asset becomes an index not of utility, but of alignment with a collective worldview.

Such alignment, however, is not always benign. There is a risk that signalling eclipses substance. Investors may chase assets not because they believe in the object itself, but because they wish to broadcast membership in a specific class. This creates a feedback loop: as more people buy in for the status, the market heats up, sometimes detached from intrinsic merit. The 2021 NFT boom demonstrated this vividly. Digital images were purchased not for aesthetic appreciation, but as digital flags—proofs of savviness, modernity, or insider status in a fast-moving world. The result was a speculative mania built less on belief in the assets themselves than on belief in the power of the signal.

To dismiss this as irrational would be simplistic. Status, after all, is not a frivolous by-product of investing; it is a form of value that affects real behaviour, influences prices, and shapes markets. The key is discernment. Knowing when a signal is built on substance—genuine cultural, historical, or aesthetic significance—and when it is built on novelty, hype, or engineered scarcity. This is where deep domain expertise becomes indispensable. A seasoned art advisor can distinguish between a historically significant piece and a derivative trend. A veteran whisky investor knows the difference between distilleries with enduring legacies and those leveraging temporary buzz.

Ethically, the signal effect also raises questions about accessibility and inequality. When value is tied to social cues and insider knowledge, markets can become exclusionary. The very mechanisms that confer prestige also gatekeep. This is particularly evident in art, where museums, galleries, and collectors create a feedback loop that determines what—and who—is deemed investable. It is a self-reinforcing ecosystem in which status accrues to those who already possess the cultural literacy required to decode it. That literacy, often the product of education, travel, and network, is not distributed equally.

Yet for all its complexities, the signal effect is not inherently problematic. In fact, it can foster greater appreciation for craft, history, and nuance. When executed with integrity and curiosity, investing in rare assets becomes a form of cultural participation. The collector who studies the evolution of watchmaking, the investor who researches independent distilleries, the patron who supports emerging artists—they are all contributing to ecosystems of meaning, not just markets. Their investments function as endorsements of quality, narratives of care, and expressions of personal philosophy.

The strategic investor, therefore, must master two languages: the language of markets and the language of symbols. Understanding liquidity, market cycles, and provenance is necessary. But understanding what an object *means*—to a subculture, a movement, a generation—is what unlocks asymmetric value. This requires immersion, not just analysis. It requires attention to aesthetics, history, and social context. It requires, in other words, cultural intelligence.

As traditional asset classes become increasingly commoditised and algorithmically traded, the premium on human judgement, taste, and discernment is rising. Rare assets—precisely because they are ambiguous, contextual, and story-laden—resist automation. Their value lives in interpretation, and interpretation cannot be outsourced. In this way, the signal effect reminds us of something deeply human about investing: that behind every decision lies a desire not just to earn, but to be seen. Not merely to possess, but to express. And in alternative markets, those expressions are not noise. They are part of the signal.

The Story Premium: Why Narrative Drives Value

Financial markets reward pattern recognition, but alternative assets reward storytelling. Investors who understand this distinction gain access to an underappreciated form of alpha—one that doesn't show up on spreadsheets but can dramatically shape asset appreciation over time. Stories, when embedded in an asset, don't just decorate it—they define it. They confer identity, frame perception, and often elevate the asset's market value beyond what its technical or material characteristics alone could command. This phenomenon—the *story premium*—is not sentimental fluff. It is a repeatable, observable economic multiplier.

A bottle of wine is not merely fermented grapes in glass. Its valuation can differ by an order of magnitude based not only on vineyard or vintage, but on the narrative surrounding it. Was the year unusually hot, producing low yields and high concentration? Was the winemaker a visionary who defied convention? Did the wine feature in a Michelin-starred restaurant's legendary tasting menu? These details do more than add flavour—they build context. And context creates conviction.

When Château Lafite Rothschild 1982 became a global phenomenon, its excellence was certainly part of the story. But it wasn't just tannin structure or aromatic depth that propelled it to mythic status. It was the tale of a breakout vintage, of Robert Parker's enthusiastic endorsement at a pivotal moment in wine criticism, of geopolitical appeal as Chinese collectors sought symbols of refinement. The wine became more than a drink—it became a narrative vehicle, carrying connotations of power, discernment, and historical timing. Its market value soared accordingly.

The same mechanics are visible in the music royalty market. Two identical catalogues, matched on earnings and genre, can diverge significantly in valuation depending on the artist's life story, cultural relevance, or lyrical backstory. A song that became a protest anthem, or featured in a generationally defining film, carries not just listening appeal but emotional equity. This kind of narrative adhesion influences institutional buyers and private investors alike. Passive income from royalties is attractive, but *meaningful* passive income—anchored to culturally resonant works—commands a premium. It is seen as less likely to decay, more likely to be rediscovered, and more deeply rooted in the public's collective memory.

Economists and behavioural scientists have long understood that humans assign value not only based on utility, but on narrative coherence. Daniel Kahneman and Amos Tversky's work on cognitive biases uncovered the "narrative fallacy"—our tendency to impose causality and order onto random events. But in the world of alternative investing, this cognitive shortcut becomes a market feature, not a flaw. Assets that *tell a good story* are perceived as safer, more memorable, and ultimately more desirable. The human brain privileges what it can remember, retell, and emotionally engage with. Narrative increases both perceived familiarity and trust—key drivers in any investment context.

This is especially true in illiquid markets, where pricing is more art than science. With no central exchange or consensus valuation, the ability to tell a compelling story about an asset often plays an outsized role in determining its price ceiling. Take the example of rare books. A signed first edition of *On the Origin of Species* by Charles Darwin is valuable not only for its scarcity, but because it connects the buyer directly to a seismic intellectual breakthrough. The book becomes a symbol of curiosity, scientific courage, and intellectual lineage. The narrative is inseparable from the object.

Contrast this with a similar-aged book of similar scarcity, but one disconnected from cultural moments or intellectual revolutions. Its value may rise slowly, if at all. This is the power of anchoring assets to significance. The same logic applies across other asset classes. A watch worn during a summit meeting between world leaders will likely outperform the identical model kept in a safe. A whisky aged during a politically tumultuous decade, or produced in tribute to a late distiller, often commands multiples over standard releases. The physical product remains similar; it is the narrative differential that investors are pricing in.

The "story premium" is not just about heritage—it is also about scarcity with context. A one-off artwork by a historically marginalised artist can suddenly reprice upward as public awareness shifts and curatorial attention reframes its significance. A sports jersey worn during a title-clinching match may spike in value not because of fabric or wear but because of moment—the convergence of time, audience, and emotional investment. These are not marginal signals. They are core economic drivers in the asset's market trajectory.

However, not all narratives confer equal weight. For a story to generate sustained economic impact, it must meet certain criteria. First, it must be *legible*—understandable by the audience without excessive interpretation. Second, it must be *transferable*—capable of being retold across contexts without losing its core appeal. Third, it must be *aligned*—consistent with the values and interests of the target market. An asset with a brilliant backstory that appeals to no one lacks market traction. But when alignment is strong—when the story resonates emotionally, culturally, or politically—it transforms the asset into a conversation piece. And conversation sustains demand.

Digital assets have provided a recent stress test of this principle. During the NFT boom, thousands of projects launched with technical novelty but minimal narrative substance. Many faded quickly. Those that endured—like the early works of Beeple or iconic CryptoPunks—did so because they accrued narrative significance. Beeple's work, for instance, was framed not merely as digital art but as a commentary on digital life, internet culture, and artistic persistence. The daily practice behind his "Everydays" series became a story of modern creative discipline. That meta-narrative allowed collectors to identify not just with the image, but with the ethos.

Even in institutional capital, story matters more than is often admitted. Private equity firms acquiring music catalogues aren't just running discounted cash flow models. They're assessing durability of brand, longevity of appeal, and social resonance. Songs written in response to pivotal moments in history—or performed by artists whose public image carries integrity—are seen as more bankable over time. This is not mysticism. It is probabilistic reasoning through the lens of narrative strength.

Yet, there is risk in over-relying on storytelling without substance. Investors must be wary of hollow narratives—stories engineered purely for marketing effect without historical or emotional weight. These narratives can inflate valuations temporarily, but lack staying power. The due diligence required in narrative-driven investing is not simply fact-checking, but *meaning-checking*: does this story connect to real cultural currents? Is it anchored in truth, or is it mere positioning? Does it evoke genuine response, or is it an exercise in style over substance?

A deeper implication of the story premium is that investors become curators. Unlike passive holders of assets, those who engage in narrative-rich investing must think about context, provenance, future interpretation, and stewardship. Buying a vineyard is not just an agricultural investment—it is an act of place-making, of sustaining tradition, of participating in a landscape of stories that predate and outlast the investor. Similarly, acquiring a legacy music catalogue is not just acquiring royalties—it is preserving fragments of the cultural record. These responsibilities are not burdens; they are value multipliers when approached with care.

The highest-functioning investors in alternative markets tend to operate like cultural historians with capital. They understand that every asset sits within a broader interpretive framework—and that being early to identify and support compelling narratives is a form of arbitrage. They see what others don't yet value. They connect the dots between past, present, and potential. And they understand that markets, ultimately, respond not just to supply and demand, but to meaning.

Narratives move markets because people move markets. And people are more captivated by stories than statistics. This is not irrationality—it is human design. To invest with narrative fluency is not to abandon rigour, but to expand it. It is to recognise that value is shaped as much by perception as by performance, and that meaning is one of the most underpriced forces in the investment world. The story premium is not a niche idea—it is a structural one.

Those who master it will not only earn returns. They will shape the cultural memory of what was worth owning.

From Utility to Symbol: The Shift in Asset Meaning

A wristwatch tells the time. A plot of farmland grows food. A bottle of wine quenches thirst. These are the original, functional roles such goods were designed to fulfil. But somewhere along the way, their meaning evolved. They began to carry messages far beyond their utility—messages about taste, legacy, heritage, even moral identity. What was once an instrument of necessity became a vessel of symbolism. In the world of alternative investments, understanding this shift from utility to symbol is not optional—it is essential to decoding how value behaves, how markets respond, and how risk is perceived.

The transformation of goods from function to symbol is not merely a philosophical point. It has direct implications for valuation, liquidity, and investor psychology. It explains why one watch can sell for £3,000 and another, functionally similar, for £300,000. It clarifies why a single hectare of vineyard in Burgundy can trade at fifty times the per-acre value of more fertile farmland elsewhere. And it reveals the crucial difference between what something *does* and what it *means*. In financial terms, that difference often accounts for the majority of an asset's premium.

Take the case of the mechanical wristwatch. As a timekeeping device, it has long been obsolete. Quartz movements are more accurate, smartwatches more functional. Yet the market for vintage and haute horology watches has never been stronger. A steel Patek Philippe Nautilus or an early Rolex Submariner—technologically unremarkable by modern standards—can command staggering prices at auction. Why? Because their worth is not rooted in utility. It is rooted in symbolism. These watches signify legacy, precision, heritage, and insider knowledge. They are worn not to tell time, but to tell *stories*—about the wearer's values, affiliations, and understanding of cultural capital.

This shift is not accidental. It is structurally engineered by brands, reinforced by collectors, and amplified by media ecosystems that thrive on scarcity and narrative. When Patek Philippe adverts proclaim, "You never actually own a Patek Philippe. You merely look after it for the next generation," they are not marketing timepieces. They are marketing the idea of time as legacy, of ownership as stewardship. The watch becomes a symbol not just of wealth, but of continuity, tradition, and familial responsibility. That's an emotional payload no spreadsheet can quantify, but it affects resale value more reliably than technical specs ever could.

Farmland presents another compelling case study. On paper, it is a productive asset—generating income through crop yields, grazing leases, or carbon offsets. But its rising appeal among high-net-worth investors cannot be explained by productivity alone. Increasingly, land is viewed symbolically: as permanence in a volatile world, as a hedge against climate anxiety, as a moral counterpoint to abstract finance. Owning farmland is no longer just about income—it's about signalling a connection to real things, to continuity, to stewardship of the Earth. This symbolism is amplified when the land is organic, regenerative, or historically significant. The return profile may remain similar, but the emotional and cultural returns increase exponentially.

The implications of this shift are multifold. First, it alters the volatility and liquidity profile of assets. Functional goods tend to trade on standardised, largely rational bases—production cost, maintenance, yield. Symbolic assets, by contrast, are more volatile, because their value is tied to perception, narrative, and cultural momentum. They are less liquid, because their buyer pool shrinks to those who understand or desire the symbolism. A classic Land Rover Defender used in a Bond film is not the same market asset as a standard production model. The former's value swings with film popularity, collector sentiment, and cultural memory. It's a risk profile rooted not in mechanical reliability, but in semiotic appeal.

Second, symbolic goods introduce a new kind of due diligence. Evaluating a vineyard's ROI is one thing; evaluating the cultural credibility of its terroir is another. Investors must now assess not only fundamentals, but *narrative positioning*: Is this asset part of a meaningful story? Will it matter in five, ten, twenty years? Does it align with evolving values around sustainability, identity, or authenticity? These questions are not marketing fluff—they are now part of intelligent asset analysis in an age where meaning and money are increasingly entangled.

This dynamic also complicates traditional notions of risk. When an asset's value is tied to symbolism, reputational risk becomes financial risk. If a revered artist becomes controversial, their market can collapse overnight. If a brand's image is tarnished, symbolic premiums evaporate. The 2017 backlash against certain fashion houses over cultural insensitivity wiped millions off their brand valuations—not because the garments stopped being wearable, but because their *meanings* became toxic. In a symbolic economy, *what an object says* is as financially consequential as what it does.

There is also an ethical dimension to this shift. As more investors pursue symbolic goods, access becomes more exclusionary. The very dynamics that elevate meaning—narrative scarcity, insider fluency, cultural cachet—also narrow the ownership field. This reinforces a hierarchy of participation in which symbolic literacy becomes a prerequisite to market entry. The result is not just wealth inequality, but *meaning inequality*: who gets to decide what counts, what matters, what should be preserved.

And yet, this very complexity is what makes symbolic assets compelling. Their richness lies in their ambiguity, their multidimensionality. A bottle of whisky is not just a consumer good—it's a node in a network of history, craftsmanship, geography, and social aspiration. A watch is not just a dial—it's a totem of class, heritage, and mechanical philosophy. These meanings shift with time, market mood, and cultural currents. That volatility is not just noise. It's part of the asset's appeal to those who seek not only financial returns, but intellectual and emotional engagement.

Some critics argue that the symbolic turn distracts from fundamentals—that it introduces irrationality into markets better governed by logic. But this is a misunderstanding. All markets are part logic, part belief. Symbolism does not erase fundamentals; it *layers over* them, influencing how those fundamentals are interpreted and priced. The astute investor recognises that utility and symbol are not mutually exclusive. They are complementary lenses. One sees what the asset does. The other sees what it *represents*—and in a culture where meaning is increasingly scarce, that second lens is often more lucrative.

This convergence of function and meaning is not confined to luxury categories. Consider sneakers—once functional athletic gear, now a £10 billion global market of collectible status items. Or farmland—once a backdrop of rural subsistence, now a portfolio staple for those wishing to hedge against collapse or virtue-signal sustainability. In each case, meaning has moved to the foreground. The objects have become narratives. And the narratives have become capital.

To invest wisely in symbolic assets, one must become a semiotician as much as a financier. This means learning to decode aesthetic signals, cultural movements, and shifting consumer values. It means tracking not just price charts, but story arcs. It means recognising that the most valuable assets of the future may not be those with the highest yield today, but those best positioned to mean something tomorrow.

The shift from utility to symbol is not a passing trend—it is a structural evolution in how capital interacts with culture. For the investor willing to think laterally, it offers an advantage rooted in insight rather than access. And for the thoughtful steward of wealth, it offers a portfolio that does more than grow. It speaks. It signals. It endures.

Chapter 2
Beyond Stocks and Bonds—The Case for Alternative Thinking

Diversification has long been treated as a near-sacred principle in investment strategy—a comforting mantra promising protection through variety, balance through allocation, and resilience through spread. Modern portfolio theory teaches that a careful mix of equities, bonds, and perhaps a sprinkling of real estate or cash equivalents will temper volatility while preserving long-term returns. For decades, this model seemed adequate. Yet recent experience has exposed its limitations. When markets fall together, diversification reveals itself as a fragile illusion. In those moments of systemic crisis, correlations surge, and portfolios built on assumptions of independence are laid bare.

This chapter opens with a challenge: the conventional notion of diversification is overstated, often misunderstood, and increasingly ineffective against global shocks and macroeconomic synchronisation. In times of financial collapse, pandemics, or geopolitical turmoil, the expected separation between asset classes vanishes. Bonds no longer reliably hedge equities. Markets that once moved in localised rhythms respond in unison to central bank signals, oil-price swings, and risk-off sentiment. Volatility becomes contagious.

The problem is not merely tactical; it is structural. Many investors are not truly diversified—they are variations on the same theme, tied to capital markets dominated by institutional flows, policy regimes, and increasingly uniform behavioural patterns. Risk is replicated, dressed in the language of modern finance, rather than genuinely mitigated. Comfort may sustain the illusion, but for those seeking resilience, it must be dismantled.

True diversification increasingly resides in the unconventional, the tangible, and the culturally embedded. It lies in assets whose value stems not from market engineering or macro cycles but from scarcity, utility, and meaning. A barrel of ageing bourbon does not track Fed commentary. An old-growth forest does not mirror the S&P 500. Music royalties, arable land, rare watches, or vintage automobiles—these respond to different forces, follow different clocks, and appeal to distinct forms of capital.

Their detachment from traditional markets is deliberate. Illiquidity, opacity, and benchmarking difficulties are not drawbacks—they are strengths. Such assets are insulated from the rapid feedback loops and herd behaviour that destabilise conventional portfolios. They inhabit slower, more culturally nuanced ecosystems where supply and demand evolve in step with human patterns of taste, use, and identity. For the discerning investor, these characteristics offer protection, not inconvenience.

Yet resilience alone does not tell the full story. Alternative assets reveal something deeper about investor priorities. Liquidity, long celebrated as a virtue, increasingly competes with legacy. Family offices, sovereign funds, and ultra-high-net-worth individuals place capital in holdings that cannot be liquidated tomorrow—not out of negligence, but because their timelines and philosophies are generational. Transactional investing gives way to intergenerational stewardship.

This shift carries profound implications. Liquidity often comes at a cost: volatility, algorithmic exposure, and behavioural traps. Illiquidity disciplines. It rewards patience, cultivates conviction, and aligns incentives with long-term value creation. A collector acquiring museum-grade art, or a trust conserving rewilding acreage, measures success not in quarterly marks but in permanence, impact, and narrative continuity. These assets are identity markers, not just financial instruments.

Indeed, for many contemporary investors, the line between asset class and identity has blurred. Capital is no longer allocated solely for returns—it expresses values, signals belonging, and constructs personal mythology. A forest, a first edition, a distillery cask, or music rights tells a story. Ownership becomes autobiographical. It declares taste, belief, and vision for the future.

This symbolic dimension is structural, not anecdotal. It reflects broader cultural currents: the rise of personal branding, the premium on tangibility and heritage, and the quest for uniqueness amid digital sameness. In this environment, portfolios are cultural artefacts as much as financial instruments. Navigating them demands literacy not only in macroeconomics and spreadsheets but also in aesthetics, history, and human psychology.

To be clear, this is not a repudiation of equities or bonds. Traditional instruments remain useful, particularly for liquidity management and institutional mandates. But they must be contextualised within a wider framework—one that recognises limitations and supplements them with assets offering depth, texture, and resilience. The goal is not diversification by category, but by worldview; not allocation by label, but allocation by meaning.

In this chapter, we dismantle the myth of uncorrelated diversification and present a more rigorous approach to resilience, grounded in asset behaviour rather than classification. We explore asset classes exhibiting genuine non-correlation—from timberland to whisky—and examine the economic, ecological, and emotional logics that drive them. We consider why leading investors increasingly favour the illiquid, idiosyncratic, and culturally resonant, and probe the intersection of money and identity: how what we own reflects not just what we can do, but who we are, and who we aspire to become.

The task is not merely to understand alternative assets as instruments of return, but as mirrors of a broader investment philosophy—one that prizes slowness in an age of acceleration, substance over scale, and alignment over mere accumulation. Alternative thinking is less a reaction to volatility than a deliberate orientation toward things that endure, resonate, and matter beyond the ticker tape.

The Myth of Diversification in a Correlated World

Diversification is one of the most repeated—and least interrogated—principles in modern investing. Almost every investment professional, wealth manager, and financial textbook touts it as a foundational rule: spread your risk across uncorrelated asset classes and your portfolio will weather volatility with grace. It sounds elegant. Rational. Empirical. But the assumption that diversification works uniformly across timeframes, markets, and crises has been cracked open in recent decades—and what spills out is discomforting. The reality is that diversification, as traditionally practised, often fails when investors need it most. And this failure is not a matter of chance. It is structural, behavioural, and increasingly predictable.

The core problem is deceptively simple: *correlation is not static.* What appears to be uncorrelated in periods of market calm often becomes tightly linked in moments of systemic stress. Asset classes that seem independent during expansionary cycles—equities and corporate bonds, developed and emerging markets, even public and private equity—frequently converge in downturns. This convergence erodes the supposed benefits of diversification precisely when protection is needed. In practice, what many investors hold is not a diversified portfolio, but a collection of different packaging around similar risk.

The 2008 global financial crisis revealed the fragility of diversification narratives on a historic scale. Portfolios that included stocks, real estate investment trusts (REITs), high-yield bonds, and commodities—all once thought to be diversifying components—sank together. Even gold, often romanticised as a crisis hedge, wobbled under the weight of a liquidity crunch before eventually recovering. The simultaneous sell-off across asset classes underscored a hard truth: when fear dominates, markets become synchronised not by fundamentals but by psychology, liquidity needs, and institutional behaviour. Diversification based on historical correlation matrices breaks down under systemic duress.

Nor was this phenomenon isolated. The COVID-19 market shock in March 2020 delivered a similar blow. Equities, corporate debt, emerging market bonds, and even parts of the Treasury market saw wild swings in the same direction. Central banks intervened with unprecedented speed and force, but the initial shock was instructive.

It revealed how closely interconnected modern financial markets have become—linked not just by capital flows, but by algorithms, leverage, and shared information ecosystems. Traditional diversification increasingly resembles a risk mirage: something that appears substantial until you need to lean on it.

Understanding this problem requires rethinking the assumptions baked into most portfolio models. The first assumption is that correlation is stable. It isn't. Correlation is highly path-dependent and regime-sensitive. It reflects market structure, investor positioning, and macroeconomic backdrop. During credit expansions, assets tend to decorrelate because optimism breeds dispersion. But under stress, behavioural synchrony takes over. Panic overrides differentiation. This is not a statistical anomaly; it is human nature expressed through capital.

The second assumption is that asset classes behave independently because they are categorically different. Yet categories are not the same as causes. Two instruments may be labelled differently—say, equities and real estate—but both can be driven by interest rates, credit conditions, and investor sentiment. If their price movements are governed by overlapping macroeconomic factors, then owning both does not truly diversify risk. It merely distributes it across different façades.

The third assumption is that diversification equals safety. This conflation is dangerous. True safety comes not from spreading exposure, but from owning assets that genuinely respond to distinct inputs—ideally inputs that are not financially engineered or emotionally reactive. It is here that alternative assets become more than a curiosity. They become a necessity.

Assets with true non-correlation behave independently because their value is governed by forces outside conventional capital markets. Consider mature barrels of bourbon. Their appreciation is driven by biological ageing, weather variability, distillery reputation, and global demand for premium spirits. These dynamics are not tethered to monetary policy or equity beta. They exist in their own cadence. Similarly, a stand of hardwood timber grows—literally—regardless of equity volatility or GDP forecasts. Trees don't check the VIX before adding a growth ring.

Farmland, too, is illustrative. While it is increasingly financialised through institutional investment vehicles, its core value derives from yield productivity, soil quality, location, and access to water. These are physical, enduring variables—not mood-based or speculative. Of course, farmland is not immune to external risks, including climate and policy. But it behaves on different timelines, with different stakeholders, and under different psychological pressures than public markets.

The advantage of these assets is not just non-correlation—it is *asymmetric correlation*. That is, their price movements tend to be stable or positively decoupled during periods when traditional assets falter. They also offer inflation sensitivity, scarcity-driven appreciation, and in many cases, tactile reassurance. Unlike digital equity tickers, they are physically present. This tangibility reinforces conviction during turbulent markets, which itself is a form of behavioural edge.

Yet investing in these unorthodox assets requires a mindset shift. The frameworks used to evaluate public market instruments—liquidity, volatility, standard deviation—don't cleanly apply. A cask of whisky has no daily mark-to-market value. A forest has no live ticker. This opacity is often cited as a weakness. But it may be a strength. In a world obsessed with instantaneous pricing, illiquidity acts as a psychological anchor. It prevents panic selling and promotes long-term thinking—qualities that diversification was supposed to cultivate but rarely does in practice.

It's also important to recognise that many alternative assets attract niche expertise. Their markets are inefficient, fragmented, and often driven by insider knowledge. For some investors, this creates friction. For others, it creates opportunity. The lack of institutional consensus means prices are not yet crowded by algorithmic trades or herd behaviour. Narrative, provenance, and scarcity still matter. This injects a layer of human judgement that, while harder to quantify, is often more durable than technical signals.

However, a critical caveat remains: not all alternatives are truly decorrelated. Cryptoassets, for example, were initially heralded as independent from traditional finance. Yet during selloffs, they often behave more like high-beta tech stocks than uncorrelated hedges. NFTs, once touted as digital diversification, largely traded on speculative momentum rather than structural independence. In practice, their correlation to investor sentiment was brutally exposed during downturns. The lesson here is that alternatives must be evaluated not by novelty, but by their *underlying price drivers*. If those drivers are behavioural, then the asset is not decorrelated. It is simply speculative by another name.

True diversification requires a return to first principles: What actually moves the value of this asset? Who holds it? What are their motivations? How fast can they sell? What psychological or structural pressures will affect their decision-making? Only by answering these questions can one build a portfolio that does not merely appear diversified but *functions* as such under stress.

The institutional investing world is slowly adapting. Endowments, sovereign wealth funds, and family offices are increasingly allocating to unlisted, tangible, and culturally specific assets. Not out of trend-chasing, but because they've seen correlation break down too many times to remain tethered to theory. Their diversification strategy is less about allocating by category and more about allocating by behaviour. What assets will behave differently *because they are fundamentally different*?

For individual investors, the implications are profound. Real diversification may involve accepting less liquidity, embracing qualitative analysis, and developing domain-specific knowledge. It may mean favouring narrative over numerical models in certain cases, or holding assets that are hard to explain but easy to believe in. This is not a departure from rigour. It is an expansion of it.

Diversification is not dead, but its lazy application is. The next generation of portfolios will not rely on a mechanical blend of stocks and bonds. They will be built on insight into how humans behave under pressure, how different systems allocate value, and how to place capital where panic cannot easily follow. In a correlated world, safety does not come from labels. It comes from independence—of value, of thought, and of conviction.

The Rise of Non-Correlation Assets

Market downturns have a unique way of revealing what matters. When asset prices fall in unison, when liquidity dries up and models begin to fray, investors rediscover—often the hard way—that correlation is the real risk multiplier. The challenge is not volatility in isolation, but the compounding effect of everything falling together. In such moments, the true value of non-correlation becomes glaringly evident. It is not just a statistical preference; it becomes a form of insurance against systemic convergence. And increasingly, this insurance is being sought not in derivatives or derivatives of derivatives, but in tangible, unorthodox, and culturally anchored assets—barrels of bourbon, tracts of timberland, vintage instruments, even arable soil.

The shift toward non-correlation assets is not simply a rejection of equities and bonds. It is a rebalancing of epistemology—a way of acknowledging that not all value is created through capital markets, and not all resilience is measured in beta. Investors are learning to differentiate between assets that *exist within the financial system* and assets that *exist outside of it*, or at least adjacent to it. This is not nostalgia for the pre-modern. It is strategic pragmatism in the face of a global system where correlation is no longer a bug—it's a feature.

Take the bourbon barrel as a case study. At first glance, it appears niche, perhaps eccentric. But look more closely, and you will find a tightly controlled supply chain, inelastic global demand, and a maturation process dictated by time, not markets. A cask of well-aged bourbon gains value not because a central bank adjusts rates, but because its flavour profile deepens, its scarcity increases, and its eventual bottling becomes part of a narrative arc consumers want to buy into. Importantly, its value is rarely affected by equity volatility. If anything, demand for prestige spirits often remains steady or increases during economic downturns, as affluent consumers shift spending from experiences to objects with perceived permanence.

This decoupling from the macro-financial cycle is not incidental—it is structural. Barrels of bourbon cannot be day-traded. Their maturation cannot be accelerated beyond what chemistry permits. There are no ETFs tracking them. Their resistance to correlation is rooted in biology, climate, and consumption, not investor sentiment or institutional flows. As a result, their price behaviour is not just different—it is differently motivated. And that difference is what makes them useful in a diversified portfolio not merely for their yield potential, but for their behavioural independence.

Now contrast this with timberland—an asset often misunderstood because it sits at the intersection of commodity production, real estate, and environmental strategy. Timberland appreciates biologically, but is also influenced by construction cycles, carbon policy, and land scarcity. Crucially, timber does not follow the same rhythm as equities. Trees do not respond to headline risk. They grow. Even when timber prices fall, the underlying biological growth continues, effectively allowing investors to wait out price troughs. This capacity for patient appreciation, coupled with the option to monetise through either harvesting or conservation, gives timberland a unique versatility. It can behave like a cash-flow asset, a real estate play, or a carbon offset vehicle depending on how it is managed.

Moreover, timberland is a long-duration asset in the truest sense. It invites a different kind of investor psychology—one that resists the high-frequency urgency of conventional markets. This patience is not just behavioural; it has financial consequences. Investors who can absorb illiquidity and allow trees to reach optimal maturity often outperform those who attempt to game the cycles. The return here is a function of biology, optionality, and time, not volatility arbitrage or beta exposure. And again, the key point: these returns have low correlation to the movements of global equity markets.

These examples are not outliers. Across asset categories, there is growing recognition that true non-correlation comes from *structural and behavioural separateness*. It comes from assets that have their own logic, their own communities of value, and their own timelines. Farmland, for instance, is increasingly attractive not just for its yield or inflation protection, but because it represents sovereignty of value. Food does not go out of fashion. The productive potential of land, especially in regions with favourable climate and water access, remains both tangible and necessary. Its value is dictated not by investor mood, but by demographic demand, soil health, and macro-trends in food systems. While land prices can be cyclical, their drivers are so different from equities that their inclusion in a portfolio genuinely broadens its behavioural profile.

The same principle applies in intellectual property. Royalty streams from books, films, and music can provide stable, often uncorrelated income flows. A 1990s hit song continues to generate royalties each time it is streamed, used in an advert, or licensed for film. These flows are not contingent on market risk appetite. They are tied to cultural relevance and consumption habits that move on separate axes from equity volatility. When structured correctly, such assets can deliver consistent cash flow with very low correlation to capital markets—especially when derived from diversified catalogues with enduring demand profiles.

But the rise of non-correlation assets is not just about protection. It is also about rediscovering investment logic that is grounded in *real-world use, cultural value, and productive function*. For too long, investors have been trained to prioritise liquidity and price visibility over substance. This has created portfolios full of paper proxies—synthetic instruments that offer exposure without engagement. Non-correlation assets push back against this abstraction. They demand specificity, knowledge, and patience. They invite the investor to understand *what* they own, *why* it holds value, and *how* that value evolves.

There is, of course, a trade-off. Many non-correlated assets are less liquid, harder to price, and require more active stewardship. They lack the instant gratification of mark-to-market reporting. But this opacity is precisely what shields them from behavioural herd effects. When assets cannot be sold instantly, they cannot be panicked out of instantly. This creates a different rhythm of ownership—one that may be slower, but also more intentional and insulated from short-termism.

As a result, the investors who are adopting non-correlation assets most effectively are those who are rethinking the entire purpose of a portfolio. For family offices, mission-driven endowments, or legacy-minded individuals, the goal is no longer just quarterly performance. It is continuity, identity, alignment. In this context, a regenerative farm or a collection of culturally significant art may serve as both a store of value and a statement of belief. And the fact that these assets are not priced daily—or don't respond to central bank commentary—is no longer a flaw. It is a feature. It means the value is embedded in something deeper than momentum.

To navigate this world, investors must broaden their skillsets. Non-correlation investing is not about trend forecasting. It is about systems thinking. It requires understanding long timelines, supply chains, cultural cycles, and environmental constraints. It requires fluency in value creation mechanisms that don't rely on sentiment, speed, or leverage. And most importantly, it requires comfort with ambiguity—the understanding that not all returns are linear, and not all risks are visible.

The broader implication is philosophical. If the 20th century investor was taught to optimise for returns per unit of risk, the 21st century investor may need to optimise for *resilience per unit of meaning*. That is: What assets will continue to matter even when markets dislocate? What forms of value will endure if liquidity dries up? What investments are grounded not just in price, but in purpose?

Non-correlation assets offer a partial answer to those questions. They are not immune to loss. They are not inherently superior. But they represent a crucial shift in how we define robustness, permanence, and independence in a world where too many portfolios are built on interlinked fragilities. The real promise of these assets lies not just in their behaviour under stress, but in what they demand of us: attention, stewardship, and a broader conception of what investing can mean.

Liquidity vs. Legacy: Rethinking Investment Priorities

Ask a typical investor what they value in a financial asset, and you're likely to hear the word *liquidity* early in the conversation. The ability to enter and exit positions quickly, to react to news, and to maintain optionality is regarded as a hallmark of prudence. Liquidity offers freedom, flexibility, and psychological comfort. But ask an ultra-high-net-worth individual—or a family office stewarding intergenerational capital—what they value, and the emphasis often shifts. For them, liquidity is not always a priority. In many cases, it is deliberately avoided. Instead, the focus turns toward longevity, influence, permanence, and meaning. In a word: *legacy*.

This is not simply a difference in temperament. It reflects a deeper divergence in investment philosophy—one shaped by time horizon, purpose, and identity. Investors operating with surplus capital and long-duration objectives are often not optimising for next quarter's returns or the ability to rebalance with ease. They are thinking in decades. They are building structures, not trades. And within that framework, illiquid assets—private businesses, land, art collections, philanthropic endowments, intellectual property, timberland, and even infrastructure—play a central role. They may not be marked to market daily, but they serve goals that are rarely measured in quarterly increments.

To understand why this shift matters, it helps to first interrogate the conventional fetishisation of liquidity. Liquidity is often portrayed as a neutral good—something all investors should prefer, all else equal. In practice, however, the premium placed on liquidity can lead to behaviours that undermine long-term outcomes. Liquid markets invite overtrading, short-termism, and emotionally driven exits. They reward noise sensitivity over conviction. For investors trying to compound capital meaningfully over time, the temptation to react becomes a tax on discipline.

By contrast, illiquid investments enforce a kind of intentionality. When capital is committed to a 10-year private equity fund, or locked into a working vineyard or woodland, the investor is structurally removed from the volatility of daily headlines. The inability to exit easily becomes a feature, not a flaw—it encourages deeper due diligence, stronger alignment with managers or partners, and more patient expectations. In this way, illiquidity is not merely tolerated; it is *strategically embraced* as a behavioural edge.

This behavioural discipline is one of the reasons why family offices have steadily increased their allocation to private and illiquid assets. They are not simply chasing yield. They are constructing ecosystems of ownership that can outlast business cycles, withstand volatility, and create enduring value across generations. These investments are often embedded in a broader narrative—of stewardship, legacy-building, or community impact. The economic returns matter, but so does the reputational and relational capital that accrues from being associated with enduring, tangible assets.

Consider farmland. To a retail investor, farmland may seem like a niche or unwieldy allocation—illiquid, weather-dependent, and geographically constrained. But to an ultra-wealthy family with an intergenerational perspective, farmland offers something few other assets can: permanence. It produces something real, sustains local economies, offers potential tax efficiencies, and increasingly aligns with ESG priorities around sustainability and food security. For investors interested in passing down not just wealth, but values, owning land becomes a way of anchoring identity to place. Liquidity, in that context, would be a distraction.

The same logic applies in the world of private collections and cultural capital. Acquiring a portfolio of museum-quality art, rare manuscripts, or historically significant artefacts is not a liquid strategy. These markets are opaque, slow-moving, and often ill-suited for financial speculation. Yet they remain central to the portfolios of some of the world's most thoughtful investors—not because they promise rapid turnover, but because they speak to *cultural continuity*. A family collection, properly managed, does more than store value. It becomes a story. A legacy. An institution in miniature.

Infrastructure and private equity present similar dynamics. When a family co-invests in a wind farm, a logistics hub, or a niche manufacturing business, the motivation is rarely pure financial arbitrage. It is about participation—having a say in shaping industries, communities, or technologies. The long lock-up periods, the capital calls, the operational complexity—all are embraced because they produce outcomes that are more durable and sometimes more defensible than those available in the public markets. The investor is not a speculator but a partner.

But embracing illiquidity also requires a shift in how risk is understood. In traditional finance, risk is often equated with volatility—the variance of returns. But for those focused on legacy, risk takes on a different character. It becomes about permanence, reputation, continuity. The question is not how bumpy the ride is, but whether the destination aligns with long-term goals. Illiquid assets may show little short-term volatility, but they carry other forms of risk: concentration, lack of price discovery, regulatory shifts, or succession challenges. These risks are real, but they are often better aligned with the strategic concerns of long-horizon investors.

There is also an ethical dimension to illiquidity that is seldom discussed. Investors who are not forced to churn assets for liquidity can afford to make choices that are aligned with values. They can invest in regenerative agriculture not because it will outperform this year, but because it reflects a commitment to ecological resilience. They can support emerging artists or unlisted companies tackling social issues, because their capital is not constrained by benchmark performance or redemption cycles. Illiquidity, in this context, is not an obstacle. It is a form of freedom—freedom to invest according to conviction rather than convenience.

That said, illiquidity is not inherently noble. It must be paired with rigour. Locking up capital without a clear thesis, governance structure, or exit strategy is not legacy-building—it is negligence. The key distinction is between *passive illiquidity*—being trapped in an underperforming or misunderstood asset—and *active illiquidity*, where capital is intentionally committed to a long-term vision with appropriate controls and flexibility. The most successful long-horizon investors are those who combine patience with precision.

It is also worth noting that illiquid investments are not exclusive to the ultra-wealthy, even if they are more prevalent at that level. Increasingly, platforms are emerging that democratise access to fractional ownership in fine art, collectable cars, farmland, and private companies. While these vehicles differ in structure and scale, they reflect a growing awareness that value need not always be liquid to be real. The trade-off remains: what is gained in potential permanence is often offset by reduced optionality. But for many, this is a fair exchange—especially in a market environment where volatility and homogeneity dominate the liquid landscape.

Ultimately, the liquidity-versus-legacy question is a proxy for a deeper inquiry: *What are we optimising for?* If the answer is speed, reactivity, or relative performance, then liquidity will remain paramount. But if the goal is continuity, influence, alignment, and intergenerational meaning, then illiquidity becomes not just tolerable but desirable. It shifts the investor from the role of trader to that of architect—designing not just portfolios, but permanence.

This is not a rejection of liquidity, but a reframing of its role. Liquidity is useful for flexibility, but it is often overvalued in proportion to its actual benefit. What illiquid assets offer is something liquidity cannot: a built-in commitment device. A psychological and structural signal that the investment is intended to endure. In a world driven by quarterly results and algorithmic reactions, that endurance is not weakness. It is strength. And for those thinking beyond their own lifetimes, it is the foundation on which legacy is built.

Asset Class or Identity Class?

Capital, at its core, is not neutral. The idea that investment decisions are purely technical—driven by return forecasts, volatility metrics, or Sharpe ratios—is intellectually appealing, but incomplete. Increasingly, where people choose to place their money reveals more than their risk tolerance or time horizon. It reveals who they think they are, what they want to be associated with, and how they wish to be perceived. In this context, certain assets stop functioning like financial products and start behaving like identity statements. They are not just stores of value—they are expressions of values. Understanding this psychological and cultural dimension is not optional for modern investors; it is critical to interpreting market behaviour, portfolio construction, and the symbolic role that ownership now plays in society.

We are witnessing a blurring of boundaries between economic utility and self-expression. When an investor chooses to allocate capital to rare watches, regenerative farmland, vintage cars, blue-chip art, or song royalties, they are not only seeking non-correlated returns or tangible yield. They are participating in a cultural act. These assets carry connotations. They signal taste, belonging, worldview. A Porsche 356 or a Patek Philippe is not simply an object—it is a cipher through which an investor projects craftsmanship, nostalgia, scarcity awareness, and discernment. The same logic applies to a collector who invests in African modernism or underground jazz catalogues. The investment is no longer purely financial—it is biographical.

This shift is partly generational. The wealth holders of the 21st century, particularly those under 50, have grown up in a culture that privileges narrative, individuality, and aesthetics. They have been shaped by branding as a mode of identity formation, by the performativity of social media, and by a pervasive consumer philosophy that says what you own says who you are. These dynamics have not disappeared with age or affluence—they have merely migrated into higher asset classes. Where one might have once expressed individuality through fashion or travel, it now manifests in portfolios. Ownership becomes a medium of self-definition.

This has real implications for asset behaviour. When capital is deployed for identity reinforcement rather than pure financial optimisation, it alters the price dynamics, hold periods, and liquidity preferences associated with that asset. Consider the art market. Works by Kehinde Wiley, Jenny Saville, or Amoako Boafo are not just evaluated for potential appreciation—they are sought out for what they communicate about the collector's alignment with issues of race, gender, or global artistic inclusion. The acquisition becomes an act of affiliation. The economic return, if it comes, is often secondary to the reputational capital the piece confers in specific social or cultural circles.

The same principle applies in the world of sustainability-aligned investments. Farmland that supports regenerative agriculture, timberland managed for carbon credits, or direct equity in clean energy start-ups are increasingly popular not just for their expected cash flows, but for the personal and ideological satisfaction they deliver. These assets serve as identity anchors—they allow the investor to say, implicitly or explicitly, *this is the kind of future I support.* Whether the investor calls it ESG, impact investing, or simply values-aligned capital, the underlying driver is not efficiency—it's coherence. The desire for one's investments to reflect one's ethics is not new, but it has become systematised in ways that now significantly influence asset pricing and demand.

What we are seeing is the emergence of *identity classes*—investments chosen not simply for their risk-return profile, but for their ability to reflect and project an individual's sense of self. This reframing challenges the traditional notion of asset classes as rigid categories defined by liquidity, income generation, or tax treatment. A whiskey cask might once have been evaluated as a luxury commodity. Today, it might function as a symbol of connoisseurship and rebellion against financial homogeneity. A rare sneaker collection might be dismissed by legacy allocators but held with conviction by those who see it as cultural capital with appreciating status. These identity classes are fluid, narrative-rich, and increasingly immune to conventional metrics.

This trend is not irrational. It is human. Behavioural finance has long documented the role of emotion, bias, and heuristics in investment decision-making. But what we are describing here is not a deviation from rationality—it is an evolution of investor motivation. The investor is no longer merely a rational actor maximising returns, but a *cultural participant* navigating a world in which ownership itself has meaning beyond economics. This has always been true to some extent—land ownership has long symbolised security, watches have long marked status—but today's proliferation of niche, identity-driven investments represents a scaling and diversification of that logic.

However, this shift also introduces new complexities. When assets serve as extensions of identity, the risk of emotional attachment increases. Investors may find it more difficult to part with holdings, even in the face of deteriorating fundamentals. They may overlook warning signs, resist diversification, or over-allocate to assets that reinforce self-image. The consequence is a potential misalignment between personal narrative and portfolio health. Emotional returns can blind an investor to financial realities. This is not a theoretical risk—it is observable in markets where cultural heat or social prestige fuels bubbles and distorts value. The art world, the collectibles boom, and certain corners of crypto markets all bear this pattern.

Yet the answer is not to retreat into clinical detachment. Rather, it is to cultivate awareness—to approach identity-driven investing with both conviction and criticality. Investors must ask: *What am I really buying here? What part of me is this investment reflecting? Am I allocating for meaning, for status, for alignment—or for return? And am I clear on the trade-offs?* These questions are not distractions from strategy. They are essential to it. A portfolio built without self-awareness risks incoherence. But one built with an understanding of the psychological and cultural motives behind ownership can be not only resilient, but resonant.

There is also a broader social function to consider. When identity flows into capital, capital flows into culture. The result is a reshaping of what gets funded, what gets preserved, and what gets left behind. Identity-driven investment helps explain the rise of patronage in contemporary art, the proliferation of niche venture funds targeting underrepresented founders, and the growing interest in archival ownership—films, recordings, manuscripts—by individuals who see themselves not just as investors, but as custodians of cultural heritage. This repositions wealth as a curatorial force. And while it introduces risks of insularity and echo chambers, it also expands the definition of capital stewardship to include taste, values, and vision.

The challenge ahead is to integrate this understanding into the practice of investing without losing rigour. Identity should not override due diligence. Taste should not substitute for thesis. But neither should these dimensions be dismissed as irrelevant or unquantifiable. The rise of identity classes in investment reflects a deeper cultural shift—away from pure optimisation and toward coherence between money and meaning. It is neither trend nor fad, but a structural evolution in the psychology of capital deployment.

As portfolios become expressions of personality, affiliation, and belief, the line between finance and narrative continues to dissolve. For the modern investor, this convergence demands not only new tools of analysis but new forms of self-interrogation. What we own no longer just grows our wealth. It increasingly defines who we are—and how we are remembered. The most astute investors will not only navigate this terrain. They will embrace it, recognising that in a crowded and commoditised world, identity itself is becoming one of the most powerful differentiators of all.

Chapter 3
Casks and Returns—Inside the Whiskey Investment Boom

A generation ago, the notion that a barrel of quietly ageing whiskey could emerge as a serious alternative investment might have seemed fanciful. Yet over the past twenty years, cask whiskey has transitioned from a niche indulgence for connoisseurs into a recognised asset class, attracting hedge funds, high-net-worth individuals, and cultural investors alike. No longer confined to tastings or specialist shelves, whiskey now circulates through auction houses, private equity portfolios, and curated collections with a seriousness once reserved for fine art or vintage automobiles. What was once merely consumed is increasingly capitalised. Behind this shift lies a complex interplay of craft, culture, and financial strategy.

At the core of whiskey investing lies a paradox: value grows while doing nothing. Time, here, is not a liability—it is the engine of appreciation. Unlike most assets, whose performance depends on human effort, market swings, or innovation, a whiskey cask's principal input is patience. The longer it matures, the richer its character becomes—chemically, aromatically, and financially. Age is both measure and mechanism. For investors wearied by digital speculation or highly correlated assets, whiskey presents a radical proposition: physical value accruing slowly, predictably, and elegantly.

Not all barrels are equal. As with a £50 bottle and a £50,000 bottle, shared categorisation masks enormous divergence in composition and context. Terroir—more often associated with wine—matters: the barley, the water source, the microclimate of maturation all shape profile and market appeal. Cask type is critical. A spirit aged in ex-sherry European oak versus first-fill American bourbon develops markedly different character, influencing both taste and valuation. Distillery reputation operates as a multiplier, elevating prices through narrative and legacy rather than intrinsic quality alone. Collectability, scarcity, and bottling history compound the intangible but economically potent value.

Savvy investors recognise whiskey as more than a drink or commodity—it is culture distilled into liquid form. A Macallan linked to a royal event, a Japanese cask from a now-defunct distillery, or a rare peated expression from Islay with a devoted following carries an aura beyond flavour. These are liquid artefacts, where desirability is shaped as much by story, context, and access as by chemical composition. Increasingly, collectors approach whiskey as others approach mid-century design or impressionist painting—not indulgence, but a demonstration of discernment.

The investment appeal extends beyond symbolism. Structurally, the market has matured: cask brokers, storage solutions, regulated exchanges, and specialist funds provide the infrastructure for serious capital. Yet complexity has grown. Storage costs, evaporation—the "angel's share"—cask management, and exit strategies must be considered. Unlike traditional assets, whiskey is perishable, not through spoilage but through a finite peak-value window. Hold too long, and a cask may become over-oaked or fall out of fashion. Timing remains paramount.

Risks are real. As the asset class grows, so do opportunities for speculation, misinformation, and fraud. Opacity and exclusivity that attract investors also create vulnerabilities. Brokers may be poorly regulated, provenance misrepresented, and appraisals inflated. Instances of casks sold multiple times or rare bottlings overstated are not unheard of. Due diligence is essential; curiosity without caution is a costly error.

New entrants may be seduced by the romance of the barrel room, the master distiller's mythology, or the language of craftsmanship. Yet successful investors balance allure with scrutiny: a forensic eye for documentation, an understanding of exit pathways, and patience to know when to hold and when to sell. Real-world stories underscore this: early believers acquiring obscure Scottish casks in the 1990s now hold assets outperforming equities, while others chasing promises of guaranteed returns have discovered untraceable or overvalued holdings. Lessons abound—timing, verification, and resisting story over substance remain paramount.

Whiskey's rise as an investment mirrors a broader cultural shift toward taste-driven assets. Unlike digital collectibles or startup shares, whiskey is materially slow: it must be stored, monitored, tasted, and eventually realised. This creates a rare intersection of human senses, time, and cultural memory with capital.

This chapter guides readers through the unique contours of the market. Beginning with fundamentals—production, maturation, valuation, and storage—it moves to strategic considerations: sourcing, exit strategies, taxation, and intermediaries. Case studies illustrate both wealth creation and cautionary missteps, providing practical lessons grounded in experience. Finally, it equips readers with the analytical tools to distinguish genuine opportunity from market theatre.

Whether considering casks for portfolio diversification, engaging with rare bottle auctions, or simply understanding how an age-old spirit became a contemporary asset class, this chapter provides the nuance, frameworks, and perspective to act with confidence. Whiskey may age quietly in warehouses, but the world around it is speaking loudly—the attentive investor is listening.

Barrels, Bonds, and Time-Held Wealth

The quietude of a whiskey cask belies the extraordinary value it may come to represent. Resting in warehouse darkness, exposed to temperature shifts and subtle interaction with wood, the spirit evolves over time—not simply maturing chemically, but economically. Unlike many financial instruments, whiskey is not marked to market every second. Its value accumulates in months and years, not milliseconds. This temporal pacing, coupled with cultural cachet and tangible scarcity, makes whiskey—particularly aged casks—one of the most distinct and increasingly appealing alternative investments in today's asset landscape. But to treat it simply as a novelty or curiosity is to misunderstand the complexity underpinning this market. It is not enough to know that whiskey ages; one must understand *how* it ages, *what* it ages in, and *where* it ages to grasp why investors around the world are allocating serious capital to liquid in oak.

Whiskey investment pivots around a deceptively simple principle: time enhances both taste and value. The maturation process is not an afterthought; it is the essence of whiskey's identity and its pricing power. Unlike wine, which may continue to evolve in the bottle, whiskey only matures while in the cask. Once bottled, the ageing halts. This means that unbottled stock represents a living, appreciating asset—one that improves with time but is also subject to market conditions, brand reputation, and investor perception. In traditional finance, compounding occurs through reinvestment of earnings. In whiskey, it occurs through molecular exchange between spirit and stave—vanillins, tannins, lignin, and lactones shifting subtly to produce depth, smoothness, and complexity. The economics of flavour and the dynamics of scarcity converge here in a way few other assets can replicate.

Understanding the mechanics of cask variation is foundational to serious whiskey investing. Casks are not uniform vessels. They vary by size, wood type, previous contents, and cooperage quality—all of which leave an indelible mark on the spirit. A first-fill ex-sherry European oak butt will lend rich, spicy notes and command a premium in the resale market, especially for Scotch matured in such casks. By contrast, a second- or third-fill ex-bourbon American oak barrel may be more subtle in influence and may require a longer maturation period to achieve equivalent complexity. These are not trivial distinctions—they directly affect the eventual nose, palate, and perceived collectability of the whiskey, and thus its market value. The informed investor evaluates not only age and ABV, but the wood lineage and fill history of the barrel.

Distillery pedigree further drives pricing differentials, often dramatically. Brands with storied legacies and limited production runs—such as The Macallan, GlenDronach, or Karuizawa—benefit from reputational capital that can lift cask prices exponentially.

Investors are not simply buying the liquid—they are buying association with a brand narrative that has global cultural traction. This mirrors dynamics in the art world, where provenance and name recognition play decisive roles. An 18-year-old cask from a top-tier distillery might be worth several times more than a similar-aged cask from an obscure or closed operation, even if the liquid quality is objectively comparable. That said, contrarian investors sometimes seek underappreciated distilleries with improving reputations—a form of value investing within the whiskey space.

Geography matters too. Scotch whisky from the Highlands carries different connotations, maturation curves, and regulatory frameworks than Irish whiskey, Japanese whisky, or American bourbon. Regional climate influences evaporation rates—known as the "angel's share"—which impacts both the volume and character of the maturing liquid. Warmer climates accelerate interaction between spirit and cask but risk faster volume loss. Cooler, more humid environments slow this process but produce different flavour evolutions. These geographical considerations, once of interest only to distillers and blenders, are now being studied by asset managers seeking to understand yield projections and exit timing.

Investing in whiskey also requires familiarity with the stages of the cask lifecycle and the exit options available at each phase. A newly filled cask may appreciate significantly over its first five years due to early maturation and rising demand. But the value curve may flatten or even decline if held beyond its peak flavour profile unless bottled, blended, or re-casked. Some investors opt to bottle and sell directly under bespoke labels, engaging in brand creation and marketing. Others exit through brokered resale, targeting collectors or independent bottlers. Each route carries differing risk profiles, regulatory burdens, and profit potential. Unlike equities or bonds, whiskey cannot be easily marked to market; valuation is inherently interpretive, reliant on recent comparable sales, expert appraisals, and brand sentiment.

That interpretive nature is both opportunity and vulnerability. The absence of a centralised exchange or price index means information asymmetry is high. A cask's value can swing significantly depending on its documentation, warehousing location, and the perceived credibility of the seller. This creates room for arbitrage—but also for abuse. As such, rigorous due diligence is non-negotiable. Investors must verify ownership title, storage conditions, distillery confirmation, and sampling rights. Reputable brokers often provide regular condition reports, updated tasting notes, and third-party authentication. Without these, what appears to be an appreciating asset may in fact be a liability—overpriced, improperly stored, or legally encumbered.

Yet it is precisely this asymmetry—this blend of opacity and romance—that attracts a certain class of investor. Ultra-high-net-worth individuals and family offices, in particular, are drawn to assets that combine cultural capital with asymmetric upside. Whiskey's alignment with themes of patience, legacy, craftsmanship, and scarcity make it psychologically and philosophically resonant. It is illiquid, yes—but intentionally so. It discourages reactive trading, rewards those with long-term conviction, and offers tangible pleasure along the way. A cask is not just a line item; it is a sensory and narrative experience that matures quietly while portfolios fluctuate noisily elsewhere.

There is also a macroeconomic rationale for this enthusiasm. As traditional financial markets have become more volatile and more correlated, allocators are searching for assets that move to a different rhythm. Whiskey, like fine wine or vintage watches, often behaves counter-cyclically—holding or increasing value during downturns due to its tangible scarcity and affluent buyer base. Moreover, it benefits from globalisation of taste. The rise of whiskey appreciation in Asia, the Middle East, and parts of Africa has expanded the collector and consumer base well beyond the Anglo-American sphere. This growing global demand adds resilience to the asset class and opens up future liquidity pathways.

Still, this is not an unregulated frontier. Various jurisdictions impose specific tax and alcohol warehousing rules. In the UK, casks must be stored in bonded warehouses under HMRC oversight, and investors may face different VAT implications depending on their exit method. In the US, bourbon cask ownership is subject to a different legal and regulatory landscape. Understanding these subtleties is essential not only for compliance but for optimising net return. More sophisticated investors are beginning to work with legal and tax advisors to structure whiskey investments through limited partnerships or private investment vehicles to manage risk and streamline operations.

Finally, one must acknowledge that whiskey investing appeals to a particular investor psychology—those who value control over pace, craft over speed, and legacy over liquidity. It is not suitable for short-term speculators or passive asset accumulators. Rather, it rewards the collector's mindset: the ability to appreciate nuance, tolerate uncertainty, and find meaning in the tactile and the temporal. A whiskey cask is not merely a barrel; it is a slow-burning thesis—a belief that patience, scarcity, and story still have a place in capital markets.

For those who grasp this interplay—between chemistry and finance, taste and time—the whiskey cask becomes more than an object of curiosity. It becomes a portfolio anchor with soul, a hedge wrapped in heritage. And in a world increasingly defined by velocity, investing in something that only improves by waiting feels not just novel, but essential.

The Anatomy of a Bottle's Worth

Why does one bottle of whisky fetch $50 on a retail shelf while another, sealed in a wooden display box and escorted by provenance documents, commands $50,000 at auction? The difference is not merely one of age or alcohol content. It is a composite valuation—a confluence of tangible and intangible attributes ranging from the chemistry of the liquid to the mythology surrounding its origin. In the world of whisky, price is not solely about flavour; it's about *meaning*, *rarity*, *prestige*, and *story*. For the serious investor or discerning collector, understanding the anatomy of a bottle's worth is essential not only for capital allocation but for cultural literacy in a market where emotion, history, and market dynamics intersect.

At the most foundational level, *terroir* sets the stage. Borrowed from the lexicon of viticulture, terroir refers to the influence of geography, climate, water source, and local microflora on the character of the whisky. While Scotland may not speak of terroir as vocally as Burgundy does, the regional distinctions between Islay's smoky peat, Speyside's orchard fruit elegance, and Highland's robust spice are deeply tied to environmental variables. Japanese distillers, too, have built entire brands on microclimatic refinement. The Yamazaki distillery, for example, benefits from a humid, misty valley once favoured by tea masters—conditions that yield soft, rounded whiskies with a cult following. Investors who understand terroir are better positioned to identify bottles with unique profiles that stand apart in an increasingly homogenised global market.

Yet terroir alone does not explain exponential price gaps. Age is often the next variable cited, and indeed, it plays a significant role—though not always in the ways one might expect. Older whiskies are rarer by definition: cask evaporation (the "angel's share") reduces yield, and few distilleries anticipated modern-day demand in their output projections 30 years ago. A 40-year-old single malt, particularly from a closed distillery, is not just a mature spirit—it is an economic artefact. But it would be misleading to assume a linear relationship between age and value. Some 18-year-olds from prestigious distilleries outprice less-renowned 25-year-olds. This suggests that *exclusivity*, rather than age alone, plays the dominant role in the upper tiers of valuation.

Exclusivity manifests in several forms: limited editions, single-cask bottlings, discontinued lines, or expressions tied to significant cultural moments. Consider the meteoric rise of The Macallan's Fine & Rare collection. Individual bottles, aged for decades and released in annual micro-lots, routinely surpass six-figure valuations—not merely because of age or taste, but because they're embedded within a deliberately curated mythology of scarcity and elegance. The packaging is part of the value proposition: bespoke glass, embossed labels, hand-numbered details, and archival-grade boxes signal not just luxury, but custodianship. Buyers aren't just purchasing whisky; they're acquiring a status symbol designed to sit comfortably alongside rare art, watches, and vintage automobiles.

Brand reputation forms another pillar of valuation—though it is often misunderstood as a static attribute. Brands are not monoliths. They fluctuate in cultural cachet depending on distribution strategy, awards, critical reception, and collector sentiment. Distilleries such as Karuizawa, mothballed in the early 2000s, have seen their posthumous reputation rise spectacularly. Bottles that once languished on shelves are now investor darlings. The logic is clear: no new stock will ever be produced. Scarcity is permanent, which in a world addicted to the "limited edition" can create near-religious fervour. Investors must be attuned not only to production volumes but to brand trajectories and historical discontinuities.

But perhaps the most powerful variable—the one that converts a good bottle into a legendary one—is *cultural resonance.* Certain whiskies achieve mythic status not because of their age or even their flavour, but because they are tethered to collective memory. Take, for instance, the bottle released by Glenfiddich to commemorate the company's 125th anniversary. Or the Ardbeg Galileo, named after the famed astronomer and tied to a branding campaign involving actual whisky samples being sent into space. These narratives transform products into touchstones. They link the mundane act of drinking with the abstract experience of identity, history, or innovation. In economic terms, this is where the "story premium" kicks in—an intangible multiplier effect that elevates the price far beyond production cost.

Investors should not underestimate the impact of *market psychology* in this valuation process. Just as equities trade on narrative as much as earnings, whisky bottles trade on perceived momentum, scarcity hype, and cultural temperature. Secondary market auctions, particularly through platforms like Sotheby's, Bonhams, or Whisky Auctioneer, reflect a dynamic mix of speculation and sentiment. A bottle may triple in price within months if a prominent collector or celebrity is seen showcasing it, or if it wins a significant tasting award. This volatility is not necessarily irrational—it's the result of a market that blends luxury, collectability, and personal meaning in a uniquely combustible ratio.

This subjectivity also opens the door to regional preference cycles. For instance, Taiwan and Hong Kong have long been major consumers of high-end Scotch, with buyers in those markets favouring sherried expressions with rich, sweet profiles. Meanwhile, collectors in the United States may prioritise high-proof bourbons or Japanese single malts. Emerging wealth in markets such as India, Vietnam, and parts of Africa is creating new centres of demand, each with distinct taste preferences and investment behaviours. A bottle with middling traction in Europe might be a coveted prize in Lagos or Hanoi. Price, in this context, is less a function of universal quality and more a reflection of where demand coalesces across cultural and economic boundaries.

Packaging, while often dismissed as superficial, can meaningfully affect resale value. The presence of the original box, label integrity, and even the clarity of the capsule seal all factor into auction pricing. The whisky itself may be identical, but presentation cues confidence and completeness—essential in a market where buyers are often at a distance and reliant on photographic verification. This explains why some investors take elaborate care in storage and insurance, treating their whisky portfolios with the same meticulous attention as fine jewellery or contemporary art. The line between collector and custodian blurs quickly in this space.

Still, the anatomy of a bottle's worth cannot be fully understood without acknowledging risk. Not all aged whiskies appreciate. Not all limited editions hold value. The market has seen speculative bubbles, questionable third-party bottlings, and even counterfeit releases designed to mimic high-value bottles. Provenance tracking and verification have become increasingly important. Digital tools such as blockchain-anchored authenticity certificates and tamper-proof seals are being introduced by some distilleries to protect against fraud. For the investor, knowing the mechanics of the bottle's valuation is no longer optional—it is a prerequisite to participation in a maturing yet opaque market.

At its most elemental, a $50,000 whisky bottle is not a beverage—it is a vessel of trust. Trust that the age is authentic, that the distillery's reputation will endure, that the packaging is unaltered, and that there will be future buyers who see the same—or greater—value. It is this complex web of chemistry, craftsmanship, story, and signal that justifies its price. And while taste still matters, it is often the least visible component in determining worth. As with many alternative assets, the value lies less in consumption than in what the asset says about the owner, the market, and the time in which both exist.

For the thoughtful investor, then, evaluating a bottle's worth is not about chasing the highest age statement or the glossiest label. It is about decoding the multilayered interplay between scarcity, narrative, reputation, and demand—while acknowledging that none of these remain static. It is about seeing beyond the liquid and into the market's imagination. Because in whisky, as in art, the greatest premiums are reserved not for what something *is*, but for what it *means*.

Tales from the Barrel Room

Fortunes are not always built in banks or boardrooms. Sometimes, they begin in the quiet, cool stillness of a barrel room—where casks of amber liquid rest in silence, gaining character, value, and mystique.

For the discerning investor, the whiskey world is more than a niche curiosity—it's an ecosystem of craftsmanship, patience, and stories both triumphant and cautionary. While balance sheets may explain yield, they rarely capture conviction, misjudgement, or the visceral satisfaction of owning a tangible, ageing asset that whispers of history and heritage. In this section, we turn from theory to testimony—from analysis to narrative—by examining real people who've walked into the whiskey market not merely to consume but to collect, speculate, preserve, and sometimes stumble.

Take the case of Charles McAlister, a retired oil executive from Edinburgh, who made headlines when his privately held whiskey collection was valued at over £3.2 million. What began in the 1990s as a passion project—acquiring single malts during distillery tours—evolved into a disciplined accumulation strategy. McAlister wasn't just amassing bottles; he was cultivating provenance. He documented each purchase, stored every cask in temperature-controlled warehouses, and established direct relationships with Highland and Islay producers. His philosophy was guided by one principle: *treat every cask as if it were a limited-edition print from a world-renowned artist.* His collection eventually included rare Bowmore vintages and closed distillery bottlings from Port Ellen. Yet he never saw himself as a speculator. "Whiskey," he once said, "is slow capital. You have to respect the time it asks of you."

Not every story ends with an enviable portfolio. John Tran, a tech entrepreneur based in Singapore, entered the whiskey market during the boom years of 2016–2018. Attracted by headlines touting 582% growth in rare bottle values over a decade, Tran funnelled nearly $500,000 into bottles and casks sourced primarily through online brokers. What he lacked in experience, he replaced with enthusiasm—and misplaced trust. Several of the casks he purchased were later discovered to be mislabelled or housed in unlicensed storage. When he attempted to liquidate part of his holdings in 2020, he encountered opaque transfer policies, no secondary market, and logistical chaos. "I bought the story, but I skipped the footnotes," he later remarked in an investor forum. His losses were significant, but so was his lesson: without due diligence, romantic assets become expensive illusions.

Whiskey investing's appeal lies partly in its resistance to financial abstraction. It's not a ticker symbol on a screen; it's a barrel you can visit, a dram you can taste. This tangibility creates an emotional relationship with the asset—one that distillers have long understood and leveraged. Consider the GlenDoran Estate, a family-owned distillery in the Scottish Highlands, which offers fractional cask ownership bundled with immersive storytelling. Investors aren't just buying spirit; they're buying narrative. They receive annual video updates on their maturing cask, handwritten tasting notes, and invitations to seasonal gatherings. While the returns are modest, the retention rate is over 90%. As co-founder Elspeth Ross explains, "We don't sell whiskey. We sell the chance to be part of a legacy." GlenDoran's model exemplifies how emotional engagement can be monetised when it's built on transparency and trust—not just allure.

Some investors have used whiskey as a generational wealth vehicle, designing portfolios that blur the line between inheritance and investment. The Harrington family, based in Melbourne, began purchasing barrels in the early 2000s as a hedge against market volatility. Over two decades, they diversified across Scottish, Japanese, and American distilleries—focusing not only on established producers but also on emerging craft operations with limited releases. Their holdings now reside in bonded warehouses across three continents, and their children are being trained not just in the logistics of whiskey finance, but in the tasting, storage, and valuation practices that underpin its market. For the Harringtons, whiskey isn't merely an asset class—it's a curriculum. Their example underscores a key principle: when an asset carries both economic and educational value, it embeds itself deeply within family culture.

But reverence can become rigidity. Simon Leclerc, a Paris-based collector with a fondness for old Speyside bottlings, once refused an offer of €75,000 for a 1966 Macallan because he believed its "historical significance" outweighed any financial transaction. Six months later, a fire at the storage facility destroyed much of his collection, including that bottle. The insurance policy—taken out years prior—covered only 60% of its appraised value. The tragedy wasn't just monetary; it revealed the emotional inflation that often clouds judgment in alternative asset investing. Leclerc, to his credit, turned the experience into advocacy, founding a consultancy that now helps collectors insure and digitise their inventories. His story serves as a sobering reminder that passion without structure is a risk vector, not a strategy.

Perhaps one of the most striking transformations in recent whiskey investment has been the institutional shift. Once the purview of eccentric collectors and beverage connoisseurs, the space is now increasingly populated by private equity firms and investment syndicates. One such entity, CaskCore Capital, manages over £100 million in whiskey-backed assets, sourcing barrels directly from distilleries and packaging them into diversified funds. Their approach is analytic, data-driven, and relatively unromantic. According to managing director Rachel Lindholm, "We don't care if the whiskey tells a story—we care if it delivers alpha." Yet their presence has reshaped market dynamics, pushing up acquisition prices and tightening supply at the producer level. For individual investors, this institutional influx presents both an opportunity and a caution. On the one hand, it validates whiskey as a legitimate asset class. On the other, it introduces competitive pressures and pricing distortions that can displace smaller participants.

For all the spreadsheets and due diligence checklists, whiskey remains an asset imbued with the ineffable. It is not merely about age or ABV; it is about context, culture, and craftsmanship. Collectors and distillers who thrive in this space tend to combine hard-nosed pragmatism with a poetic sensibility. They know when to buy based on data—and when to hold based on instinct. They invest not only in liquid volume but in symbolic capital: the cachet of owning a pre-war Glen Grant, the honour of preserving a vanishing style, the joy of pouring a dram from a cask their grandchildren will one day inherit.

These stories from the barrel room are not outliers. They are the pulse of a market that trades in more than liquidity—it trades in time, trust, and temperament. For every investor eyeing whiskey as a financial instrument, these lessons offer grounding. For every collector intoxicated by rarity, they offer caution. And for everyone navigating this unique terrain, they offer the one thing that no index can price but every great asset demands: perspective.

Risks in a Glass: Fraud, Fakes, and Forecasts

The whiskey investment market, once defined by connoisseurship and trust, is now navigating an increasingly complex and often perilous frontier. What was once a quiet niche populated by collectors and patient speculators has, in recent years, become a global multi-billion-pound arena attracting hedge funds, syndicates, and opportunistic middlemen. With the influx of capital and media attention has come a darker parallel: the sharp rise in counterfeit bottles, fraudulent cask schemes, opaque storage arrangements, and inflated appraisals. Whiskey may mature slowly, but deception travels fast. For investors—novice or seasoned—the glass is no longer merely half full or half empty; it may be filled with risk masked as reward.

One of the most notorious cases in recent years involved a bottle of 1878 Macallan sold for $10,000 in Switzerland and later revealed to be a modern concoction of blended Scotch, caramel colouring, and grain alcohol. The incident, which garnered international headlines in 2018, was not an anomaly—it was a canary in the cask. Forensic testing by the University of Oxford using carbon dating revealed that the whisky in question could not have been distilled before 1970. While most investors are unlikely to encounter forgeries of this vintage or value, the principle remains universal: *rarity attracts scrutiny, but also deceit.*

The rise in fraud is not limited to collectible bottles. Cask investment scams have become increasingly sophisticated, preying on the allure of exclusivity and the opacity of the supply chain. In the UK, authorities have issued warnings about unregulated firms offering high-yield whiskey investments, often promising guaranteed returns within a fixed time frame—an immediate red flag in any illiquid market. Some schemes involve selling fractional ownership of barrels stored in bonded warehouses, but with little recourse to verify the cask's existence, let alone the investor's legal claim. The regulatory vacuum in this area allows unscrupulous actors to exploit novice investors under the guise of tradition, craftsmanship, and scarcity.

To understand the anatomy of a whiskey scam, one must follow the asset from grain to glass. Unlike publicly traded securities, whiskey casks lack a central registry. Most distilleries do not directly sell to the public, relying instead on brokers or independent bottlers. When an intermediary offers a "private cask" opportunity, the buyer must determine whether the seller has legitimate title, whether the warehouse contract exists in their name, and whether the cask is properly insured and stored under compliant conditions. Too often, investors receive glossy documentation but no access to physical verification. *In a market where age equals value, the paper trail is your only proof of provenance.*

Authentication remains a critical frontier. In the world of high-value bottles, chemical analysis is increasingly paired with cork, label, and capsule forensics. Independent experts like Rare Whisky 101 and consultants in Scotland now use spectroscopy and isotope profiling to determine whether the liquid matches the stated age and region. But for most investors, the solution lies in pre-emptive diligence rather than post-hoc testing. Reputable brokers should offer certificates of authenticity issued by the distillery itself, with matching warehouse receipts and unique cask numbers. If these are unavailable, the risk of misrepresentation climbs sharply.

But even well-intentioned investments are not immune to structural risk. Whiskey, like wine, matures—up to a point. Beyond certain thresholds, it deteriorates. Investors who believe that a 40-year cask is always more valuable than a 20-year one misunderstand the chemistry of maturation. Once alcohol content drops below 40% ABV due to evaporation (commonly referred to as the "angel's share"), the spirit may no longer be legally classified as whisky under Scottish law. Some private investors, unaware of this technicality, have found themselves holding barrels that are effectively unsellable. *An ageing asset can become a wasting one without a planned exit strategy.*

Forecasting returns in this category is also fraught with misunderstanding. Past performance, often cited from Knight Frank's Luxury Investment Index or Rare Whisky 101's bottle tracking reports, has been strong—but not without volatility. Bottles that fetched record prices in 2019 saw a retreat during the COVID-19 pandemic, with some segments losing liquidity altogether. This variability underscores a broader truth: alternative assets are not merely volatile—they are opaque. Without transparent markets, pricing becomes susceptible to hype, anecdote, and manipulation. A bottle sold at auction for £20,000 may make headlines, but unless it represents a broader shift in market valuation, it remains anecdotal rather than indicative.

The emotional pull of whiskey further complicates rational judgement. Investors are often driven by more than numbers—they are seduced by narrative, aesthetics, and legacy. Scammers understand this psychological landscape intimately. They craft stories around "lost recipes," "family-run distilleries," or "secret releases," knowing that investors are not merely seeking yield—they are seeking belonging. Emotional resonance can be a powerful asset in alternative investing; it can also be a dangerous liability when left unchecked by analysis. *Discernment, not sentiment, should guide entry into this market.*

That said, the solution is not to retreat, but to approach with discipline. The most successful investors in whiskey apply the same rigour they would to venture capital, real estate, or private equity. They ask for documentation. They visit warehouses. They hire third-party experts. They understand the tax implications, storage costs, and resale constraints before committing capital. They do not conflate the pleasure of ownership with the presumption of appreciation.

Importantly, the infrastructure around whiskey investment is maturing, though not without growing pains. Platforms like WhiskyInvestDirect offer more institutional-like access with standardised reporting and pooled ownership structures. Distilleries themselves are becoming more transparent, offering direct investment opportunities with detailed contracts, oversight, and exit mechanisms. Some are even exploring blockchain-based authentication tools to create immutable records of ownership—a development that could radically improve the integrity of the secondary market.

Still, caution must prevail. Just as the 2008 financial crisis revealed the dangers of complex derivatives cloaked in simplicity, whiskey's rise as a financial asset reveals the perils of romance cloaked as rigour. The value of a cask may lie not only in its flavour profile or market rarity, but in the trustworthiness of the parties transacting it. When regulators, insurers, and brokers operate in fragmented or poorly policed jurisdictions, investors bear the burden of self-protection.

Perhaps the most telling insight comes from a distiller in Campbeltown who, when asked whether he thought whiskey should be treated as an investment at all, responded dryly: "It can be. But remember, you can't drink a stock certificate when it goes wrong." His comment is more than just quip; it's a reminder that whiskey, unlike most assets, is consumable. Its value exists on a spectrum between enjoyment and economics. The risk, therefore, is not only fraud—it's forgetting why the asset matters in the first place.

To invest wisely in whiskey today is to straddle that tension: between scarcity and speculation, between tradition and disruption, between passion and prudence. The fraudsters thrive where clarity falters. But with a clear-eyed, critical approach—one grounded in verification, realism, and intellectual humility—investors can navigate this maturing market with confidence, caution, and conviction.

Chapter 4
Sound Money—Investing in Music and Book Royalties

A subtle but profound shift is underway in investing, one that has little to do with stocks, cryptocurrencies, or traditional commodities. Instead, it begins in the spheres of music, literature, streaming platforms, and licensing agreements—where culture and cash flow intersect with surprising resilience. Royalty-based investing, long the preserve of record labels, publishers, and rights lawyers, is emerging as a legitimate asset class. In an era of market volatility and diminishing returns from conventional income streams, royalties offer something increasingly rare: recurring, non-correlated, and identity-rich cash flow.

To label royalties as merely "alternative" feels outdated. When Bob Dylan sold his song catalogue to Universal Music Publishing Group for a reported $300 million, or when Taylor Swift began re-recording her early albums to reclaim master ownership, these were not simply celebrity headlines—they were indicators of a broader trend: intellectual property is becoming institutional. It is now priced, packaged, and pursued with the seriousness traditionally reserved for real estate or infrastructure. The once-muted hum of a royalty statement has become a chorus of strategic opportunity.

This chapter examines that evolution with an analytical eye. Investing in royalties is not a matter of chasing hits or nostalgia; it requires understanding contracts, territorial rights, reversion clauses, and usage patterns. It demands insight into why certain songs generate reliable income for decades while others fade after a single year, and why a midlist author may outperform a Grammy-winning musician depending on the intellectual property's structure. In this world, sound money is not simply an echo of popularity—it is a framework for viewing culture as compounding wealth.

At its simplest, a royalty is a payment to the intellectual property owner for the right to exploit that property. Yet beneath this simplicity lies considerable complexity. In music, mechanical royalties are earned through reproduction—CDs or digital downloads—performance royalties accrue when a song is broadcast or streamed, and synchronisation royalties arise when music is used in films, adverts, or other visual media. Each stream involves distinct collection societies, payout schedules, and market dynamics. For investors, success depends not only on yield but on the composition of the royalty stream—its diversification, territorial coverage, and administrative efficiency.

Consider "Every Breath You Take" by The Police. Written in 1983, it reportedly continues to generate over $2,000 a day in royalties nearly forty years later, thanks to repeated usage in films, advertisements, cover versions, and samples such as Puff Daddy's "I'll Be Missing You." Compare that to a fleeting viral hit on TikTok: hundreds of millions of streams may accumulate in weeks, yet its revenue evaporates quickly. Royalty investing rewards durability over flash.

The book market operates under analogous but nuanced principles. Traditional publishing contracts allocate royalties by format—hardcover, paperback, ebook, audiobook—as well as by territory and subsidiary rights such as film adaptations or translations. An internationally appealing nonfiction work may outperform a domestically popular bestseller, and authors who retain or reclaim rights can monetise anew through self-publishing or licensing. For investors, the critical question is the breadth of the copyright and how actively it is exploited.

Private markets have responded. Platforms such as Royalty Exchange, SongVest, and ANote Music now democratise access, allowing individuals and institutions to bid on portions of existing royalty streams. Some offer limited-term income rights, others include ownership of the underlying intellectual property. Liquidity, once scarce in this fragmented market, is growing. While risks remain, this development reframes the notion of ownership: one need not create the work to benefit from it—one must simply understand its revenue logic and price it astutely.

Royalties are particularly attractive for their relative independence from economic cycles. Music is streamed, books are read, and content consumed, even during recessions. Well-curated intellectual property can stabilise portfolios otherwise exposed to market beta. Institutional players, such as Blackstone and Hipgnosis, position royalties as inflation-resistant alternatives to bonds, drawing a parallel to toll roads or utilities: predictable income derived from habitual human behaviour. Cultural consumption rarely pauses when the economy falters; in fact, it often intensifies.

Yet this opportunity demands careful scrutiny. Not all royalties are equal: some feature declining trajectories, front-loaded payouts, or unclear chain-of-title. Catalogues may suffer from incomplete metadata, registration gaps, or opaque collection structures. Secondary and tertiary acquisitions carry counterparty risk. Technological shifts—changes to streaming algorithms, licensing laws, or platform payouts—can dramatically alter income profiles. Due diligence extends beyond projected returns into legal clarity, technological context, and cultural longevity.

This chapter also considers who is buying and why. Private equity acquisitions of music catalogues signal belief in intellectual property as predictable revenue engines with optionality: licensing, bundling, resale, and securitisation. Artists may liquidate for cash, tax strategies, or risk management; funds acquire yield alongside appreciation potential. Yet such commodification raises questions: when creativity is reduced to spreadsheets, how do we value originality? Are we investing in culture, or merely harvesting it?

Case studies—from landmark song acquisitions to lesser-known literary rights—illustrate how properly structured cultural value becomes financial value. They reveal that timing, negotiation, and strategy often outweigh mere popularity. They illuminate the delicate interplay between art and commerce, reminding readers that royalties are streams of income, yes—but also rivers of meaning. Ownership, in this context, encompasses resonance as much as rights.

As capital increasingly flows into intangible domains, scarcity is being redefined. Royalties represent scarcity grounded not in finite supply but in cultural imprint, rewarding originality, endurance, and emotional connection. To invest in royalties is not simply to chase returns; it is to participate in the financial afterlife of human expression.

This chapter equips readers with frameworks, tools, and insights for navigating this terrain. From understanding royalty structures, to evaluating viable catalogues, to recognising macro trends reshaping the industry, we map the path from sound to substance—demonstrating why the most discerning investors are learning to listen closely, for the smartest money is no longer silent.

The New Dividend: Royalties as Cash Flow

When most people imagine earning passive income, they picture a dividend cheque from a blue-chip stock or a coupon payment from a corporate bond. But increasingly, sophisticated investors are turning their attention to a different class of yield—one that's rooted not in commodities or equity markets, but in the recurring revenues of intellectual property. Royalties, particularly from music and books, represent one of the few truly non-correlated, cash-flowing assets available to private investors. They don't depend on equity valuations, interest rates, or geopolitical sentiment. Instead, they flow with human culture—triggered by the replay of a favourite song, the adaptation of a novel, or the licensing of a chorus in a TV ad. In short, royalties offer a new kind of dividend: cultural, compounding, and commercially resilient.

To understand royalty investing, one must first grasp the mechanisms of licensing. Unlike traditional income-producing assets, royalties are earned not by owning a piece of infrastructure or a share in a company, but by holding rights to intellectual property that someone else continues to monetise. For music, this might mean owning the publishing rights to a song that generates payments whenever it is streamed, broadcast, performed live, or synchronised with visual media. For books, it could mean receiving a cut every time a title is sold, translated, optioned, or adapted. The common thread is contractual entitlement to a portion of future revenue, usually over a fixed term or, in some cases, in perpetuity.

Licensing frameworks are not uniform, and this complexity is one reason the royalty market remains underappreciated by traditional investors. In music, for example, royalties are split across multiple stakeholders. A single hit track can generate several types of income: *mechanical royalties* (from physical and digital reproduction), *performance royalties* (from public broadcast or play), and *synchronisation fees* (for pairing music with film, TV, or advertising). Each stream is governed by different rights structures and collected by distinct organisations—such as PRS for Music in the UK or BMI in the United States. For book royalties, the flows are generally simpler but still require an understanding of front-end advances, subsidiary rights (such as translation or audiobook deals), and the implications of licensing to third-party distributors like Amazon or Audible.

A key advantage of royalties is their asymmetrical return profile. Because the underlying asset is intangible and generally non-depreciating, costs are minimal once rights have been secured. Meanwhile, the revenue potential can spike unexpectedly—say, if a song goes viral on social media, is featured in a critically acclaimed film, or experiences renewed interest due to cultural events. This introduces an optionality element similar to owning a call option: you have limited downside (if the song or book underperforms) but potentially explosive upside. Moreover, because these revenues are generated by consumer behaviour rather than investor sentiment, they tend to exhibit extremely low correlation with equity or bond markets—a valuable feature in any portfolio seeking resilience.

This resilience, however, comes with caveats. Not every catalog or title offers predictable cash flow, and there is substantial variability in income stability. A 1990s rock band with multiple radio hits might offer far more dependable earnings than a newly released indie track, even if the latter has critical acclaim. Similarly, a backlist novel that's taught in schools or universities may offer decades of residual value, while a celebrity-authored book with high upfront sales could fade quickly. The challenge for investors, then, is due diligence: understanding not just past earnings, but the factors that drive future performance. Is the work evergreen or trend-based? Is it regularly licensed internationally? Does it feature in playlists or algorithms with staying power? These are not metrics found in traditional financial statements but require a kind of cultural literacy that blends artistic sensibility with commercial foresight.

There are also broader macroeconomic signals to consider. The surge in private equity interest in music catalogues is not a fluke. Firms like Hipgnosis, Primary Wave, and Round Hill have spent hundreds of millions acquiring rights from artists such as Neil Young, Shakira, and Bob Dylan—not simply out of nostalgia, but because they recognise these works as annuity-grade assets. The logic is straightforward: streaming platforms like Spotify, Apple Music, and YouTube have transformed music consumption into a recurring, scalable business model. Each stream, no matter how small the fraction of a cent, adds up—especially across global audiences and long timeframes. The result is a monetisation engine that's remarkably granular, continuous, and difficult to replicate in other asset classes.

The same applies, with slightly different contours, in the publishing world. Literary estates such as those of Agatha Christie, Roald Dahl, and Ian Fleming continue to generate significant revenue long after the author's death. These are not merely nostalgic properties—they are brands, with merchandising potential, film adaptations, and international licensing deals that extend far beyond the printed page. Investors who understand the value of narrative IP—especially within the shifting sands of digital media consumption—are well placed to harvest income from intellectual property as effectively as one might from real estate or dividend stocks.

Still, investors must be wary of opacity. Royalty cash flows can be irregular and hard to forecast without historical data. Rights ownership can be fragmented, and documentation may be inconsistent or incomplete, especially with older works. In some cases, rights disputes can significantly delay or dilute expected payments. Therefore, verification is paramount. Reputable brokers and platforms—such as Royalty Exchange, SongVest, and ANote Music—have emerged to bring more transparency and liquidity to the space. But due diligence remains highly individual. It is not enough to be enamoured by an artist or impressed by past revenue. Investors must interrogate the contract terms, audit the rights ownership, and model the income based on granular data over time.

Moreover, it is essential to differentiate between investing in royalties directly and investing in companies or funds that manage them. A publicly traded vehicle such as Hipgnosis Songs Fund or Round Hill Music Royalty Fund offers diversification and professional management but may also expose investors to broader market risks and pricing inefficiencies. Conversely, buying a slice of a specific song or book via a marketplace provides greater control and potentially higher returns—but requires deeper engagement, risk tolerance, and often a longer investment horizon.

Philosophically, royalty investing appeals to those who appreciate the long tail of cultural value. A single song might bring back memories, but a catalog is a ledger of enduring emotional connections multiplied across millions of people. This is not simply a cash flow strategy—it is a bet on the stickiness of culture, the persistence of taste, and the power of narrative and sound to echo through time. In this sense, royalties offer a kind of dual dividend: monetary and meaning-laden. They represent value not just in numerical yield but in resonance—the same insight that underpins the very thesis of this book.

As economic cycles become less predictable, and traditional income assets become increasingly homogenised or correlated, royalties present an elegant alternative: a space where commercial returns are tethered to the rhythms of real culture rather than financial abstraction. They are reminders that value doesn't only emerge from volatility or leverage but from the quiet accumulation of relevance, across decades and formats.

If investors are willing to learn the mechanics, respect the risks, and cultivate the eye for durable works, royalty investing can be more than just a niche pursuit. It can be a serious, yield-generating strategy that aligns financial intelligence with cultural discernment—a combination rare enough to be prized in any portfolio.

The Hidden Giants: Who's Buying Song Rights and Why

It would be easy to mistake the recent surge in music catalogue acquisitions as a sentimental indulgence—a parade of pop stars selling off the past for headlines and retirement security. But beneath the surface, a more sophisticated financial shift is unfolding. Blackstone, KKR, Apollo, and other heavyweight private equity firms are quietly accumulating ownership of what used to be ephemeral: melody, rhythm, and cultural memory. The rights to songs—once the domain of labels and artists—have become institutional assets, valued not just for their emotional resonance but for their dependable income, legal structure, and long-tail monetisation potential. Music rights are no longer the periphery of investment strategy. They are its avant-garde.

To understand why song rights are attracting institutional capital, it's critical to begin with how this asset class behaves. Unlike equity, music rights generate *contractually obligated cash flow*, often backed by dozens or hundreds of micro-transactions across diverse geographies and platforms. Streaming, radio airplay, sync deals with film and advertising, YouTube views, and performance royalties all feed into a basket of revenues that are *unusually predictable*, *geographically diversified*, and *non-correlated with traditional market movements*. A hit song from 1995 continues to earn in 2025—not because it's growing, but because human habits are persistent. People return to what they love, and algorithms now accelerate that tendency.

For institutional investors, this pattern resembles an asset class that has long been prized: infrastructure. Like toll roads or energy grids, music rights involve upfront capital to acquire or build, followed by long-term income with manageable costs and low volatility. Yet music has an additional quality that bridges asset and brand: *cultural durability*. A single Beatles track or a Queen anthem may generate more reliable cash flow than a mid-tier commercial building—and have a better story attached. This is not a trivial observation in a world where capital increasingly seeks yield *and* narrative.

So who, exactly, is acquiring these rights—and why now? The answer spans three main categories: institutional capital, artist-investors, and strategic industry players. Each brings different motivations, timelines, and expectations to the table.

Private equity firms are the most visible new entrants. Blackstone's $1 billion partnership with Hipgnosis Songs Capital signalled a turning point in the legitimisation of music royalties as investable, cash-generating assets. These firms are not looking for novelty—they are targeting catalogues with proven earnings, often from artists with multi-decade global appeal. Think Fleetwood Mac, Bob Dylan, or Neil Young. These are low-risk plays on consumption habits that defy demographics. By acquiring publishing rights, they gain access to mechanical and performance royalties—revenue streams that, while small individually, add up impressively at scale. The business case is clear: with the rise of streaming, music consumption has become constant, borderless, and increasingly monetised. In essence, they're buying indexed cultural utility.

Alongside institutional money are the artists themselves—those who, ironically, used to be the sellers but are now becoming buyers. Taylor Swift's well-publicised feud over the ownership of her master recordings brought public attention to a long-standing structural issue in the music industry: the disproportionate power of labels and publishers in capturing long-term value. Artists like Jay-Z, Rihanna, and BTS are increasingly building out their own music IP portfolios, often through joint ventures or media companies, in order to retain control over licensing and revenue. These are not vanity projects—they are sophisticated plays at vertically integrating creative control with capital stewardship.

The third category includes strategic acquirers within the media and entertainment industry. Companies like Concord, Reservoir Media, and Primary Wave are actively purchasing catalogues not just for the royalties, but for the licensing potential across film, television, advertising, gaming, and emerging platforms like virtual reality. For these players, a song is not just a streamable asset—it's a licensable emotion, a brand anchor, and a commercial amplifier. Their acquisitions are often driven by synergy with existing IP portfolios, merchandising strategies, or global expansion ambitions.

This convergence of interests—between yield-seeking institutions, rights-aware artists, and vertically integrated media groups—has profound implications for how music IP is valued. Historically, music publishing was an opaque business, governed by insider knowledge and asymmetrical power. Valuations were modest, and transactions often kept within tight circles. Today, we are witnessing the *financialisation of creativity*: song catalogues are being priced at multiples of annual revenue, traded on structured exchanges, and analysed with tools once reserved for real estate or private equity. In this new landscape, understanding discount rates, rights splits, and synchronisation potential is as critical as having an ear for harmony.

Yet the rush into music IP also raises important conceptual tensions. If every song becomes a financial instrument, what does this mean for the role of art in society? Critics argue that reducing culture to cash flow risks devaluing artistic integrity and homogenising creative risk. There is also the danger of short-termism: investors chasing yield may favour safe, already-proven works over nurturing new talent or experimental forms. In this context, the question becomes not just what a catalogue earns—but who controls the context of its use, and to what end.

Another point of caution concerns data integrity and risk transparency. Unlike listed equities or property, royalty income is notoriously difficult to forecast precisely. Income is affected by a host of variables: how songs are used, evolving streaming algorithms, platform payouts, changes in global copyright law, and even cultural shifts in taste. Catalogues that once yielded 8–12% annually may suddenly drop off if a key platform de-emphasises certain genres or regions. Moreover, historical earnings don't always predict future resilience. A Christmas hit may spike each December, but can also be crowded out by newer releases or media usage saturation.

This is why due diligence is paramount. For large institutional players, data aggregation and historical tracking are sophisticated—often involving proprietary analytics. For retail investors entering through marketplaces like Royalty Exchange or ANote, the risks are higher. Information asymmetry, rights ambiguity, and thin secondary markets can all affect returns. The promise of passive income must be balanced with a clear-eyed view of contractual obligations, territorial splits, and the potential for legal disputes.

What's becoming increasingly evident, however, is that intellectual property is emerging as a strategic class of asset not only because of its cash flows, but because of its strategic *optionality*. A song's value isn't just in its current earnings—it's in its potential to be remixed, sampled, licensed, revived, or reframed. In a world where attention is the scarce resource, owning the content that commands attention is not just profitable—it's *pivotal.* And as streaming platforms, content libraries, and algorithmic recommendation systems become more central to media consumption, owning input IP becomes tantamount to owning infrastructure.

This is why music is not just entertainment—it's becoming *infrastructure of emotion*. It shapes mood, memory, branding, and behaviour at scale. For investors who understand this duality—art and asset, expression and annuity—the opportunity is enormous, but not naïve. Success will come not to those who chase nostalgia, but to those who can measure resonance, project cultural stickiness, and price optionality with discipline.

In this sense, the buyers of music rights today are not simply purchasing yesterday's hits. They are building silent portfolios of cultural leverage—banks of memory that will yield dividends not only in cash, but in attention, influence, and time. And while the headlines will focus on celebrity names and billion-dollar deals, the deeper story is about how ownership is migrating. From record labels to rights funds. From artists to asset managers. From passion to protocol.

For those paying attention, this is less a trend than a redefinition: intellectual property as the new frontier of yield, legacy, and control.

From Chorus to Cash: Understanding Royalty Structures

Ask the average investor about recurring revenue, and they'll likely think of dividend stocks, rental income, or software subscriptions. Rarely does the conversation veer into the world of music royalties—a domain where passive income is generated not from owning a factory or financial instrument, but from the sustained cultural relevance of a sound. Yet in the alternative investment universe, royalty streams from music compositions, recordings, and publishing rights represent an increasingly important asset class. To participate intelligently in this space, one must understand not only the creative inputs that make a song enduring, but also the legal and commercial structures through which that song becomes monetisable. At the core of this lies an underappreciated truth: *not all royalties are created equal.* Distinct in source, behaviour, and risk, each royalty type—mechanical, performance, and synchronisation—demands its own lens of analysis. Together, they create a mosaic of revenue, one that rewards both legal clarity and cultural longevity.

To grasp the anatomy of royalty cash flows, one must begin with the concept of rights fragmentation. Each song is not a single entity but rather a bundle of intellectual property rights. At the highest level, there are two main categories: the *composition* (lyrics and melody, controlled by songwriters and music publishers), and the *sound recording* (the actual recorded performance, controlled by artists and record labels). Each of these generates different types of royalties when exploited. And crucially, they are paid by different parties, tracked through separate systems, and governed by varying contractual and statutory frameworks. What this means for the investor is simple: revenue predictability, contractual enforcement, and payout latency are not uniform across the royalty spectrum.

Start with mechanical royalties—the fees paid for the reproduction of a musical composition. Whenever a song is streamed, downloaded, or pressed to vinyl, mechanical royalties are triggered. These payments are made to songwriters and publishers by entities such as Spotify, Apple Music, and physical distributors. In the digital era, the mechanical royalty has become increasingly central, but also fraught with complexity. The U.S. Copyright Royalty Board, for instance, sets the statutory mechanical rates for streaming platforms, which means that these revenue streams can be influenced by regulatory shifts. Furthermore, collection intermediaries like the Mechanical Licensing Collective (MLC) play a pivotal role in distributing mechanicals, introducing a layer of administrative dependency. For investors, mechanical royalties can offer regular, algorithmically triggered cash flow, but are also subject to industry-specific volatility such as streaming algorithm changes, catalogue ingestion delays, or metadata mismatches.

Performance royalties, in contrast, are generated when music is broadcast or played publicly—on radio stations, in restaurants, via television, or live at festivals. These royalties accrue to both the composer and the publisher, but not the performer unless the artist is also the writer. Collection societies such as ASCAP, BMI (in the U.S.), and PRS (in the U.K.) handle these payments. The advantage here is durability: classic songs that become wedding staples, radio favourites, or part of holiday playlists can produce revenue for decades, long after their initial commercial peak. For example, Mariah Carey's "All I Want for Christmas Is You" reportedly generates millions annually in performance royalties more than two decades after its release. However, investors must note that performance royalties often exhibit delayed payout cycles, with income distributed quarterly or even semi-annually. They also tend to be affected by macroeconomic forces—such as advertising budgets and leisure venue activity—which makes them less stable than their automated mechanical counterparts.

Then there is synchronisation—or "sync"—royalties, which arise when a song is licensed for visual media: films, television shows, commercials, video games, and even user-generated online content. Sync royalties can be especially lucrative. A single placement in a hit Netflix series or a viral Super Bowl ad can yield five to six figures in a one-off payment. Moreover, sync deals confer cultural prestige, often triggering a halo effect that lifts performance and streaming income as audiences rediscover the track. Consider how Fleetwood Mac's "Dreams" saw a 374% spike in streams after a viral TikTok video featuring the song went global. However, sync revenue is unpredictable. Unlike mechanical or performance royalties, it is not passive or programmatic—it depends on active deal-making, the quality of relationships with music supervisors, and the zeitgeist appeal of the underlying catalogue. For investors, sync is a bonus rather than a baseline—a potential windfall that should not be relied upon for consistent cash flow.

The legal complexity of royalty splits also deserves attention. Most compositions are co-written, with fractional ownership divided across songwriters, producers, and publishers. Without precise documentation—such as split sheets and work registrations—disputes over ownership can delay payments or invite litigation. Moreover, many catalogues suffer from rights confusion across jurisdictions, particularly when tracks span multiple countries with different collection regimes. This means investors must conduct rigorous due diligence on provenance, contractual clarity, and metadata hygiene before acquisition. Reputable catalogues often have their rights managed by experienced publishers or administration companies with global reach and accurate tracking systems. Inferior catalogues, by contrast, may sit on latent income due to rights fragmentation or misregistration.

Predictability, therefore, hinges not only on the historical earnings of a catalogue but on the systemic quality of its administration. Two catalogues may generate £50,000 in annual income, yet only one may maintain consistency due to stable licensing, geographic breadth, and ongoing relevance. Investors should examine rolling five-year earnings, seasonal spikes, and decay curves. A catalogue that relies on one hit song for 80% of its income may be far riskier than one with 40 moderate earners. This is particularly true in genres with fast trend cycles, such as pop and hip-hop, versus those with slower cultural depreciation, such as jazz, country, or adult contemporary.

Moreover, royalty investing is not immune to platform risk. As streaming continues to dominate, the concentration of revenue among a handful of platforms raises concerns. If Spotify or YouTube alters its payout formula, it could significantly affect downstream income. Similarly, geopolitical tensions and regulatory crackdowns on digital advertising or copyright enforcement could impact royalty flows across borders. This makes geographic diversity within a catalogue—songs that earn in Europe, North America, Asia, and Latin America—a key factor in risk mitigation. It also elevates the role of cross-platform licensing strength: songs that generate income across streaming, broadcast, retail, and live settings offer a more resilient income profile.

Ethical reflection is also warranted. Investing in cultural output carries reputational implications. Catalogues tied to controversial artists or offensive content may face backlash or deplatforming. Conversely, acquiring the rights to socially resonant or historically significant works—such as protest songs, film scores, or educational children's content—can generate both financial and cultural capital. Some investors intentionally curate "impact catalogues" to align financial return with social legacy, favouring works with long-term educational or civic relevance.

Finally, it is worth distinguishing between acquisition and participation. Some investors prefer outright catalogue purchases, seeking complete control over royalty flows. Others favour fractional investments via royalty exchange platforms, which offer exposure to individual songs or portions of catalogues without the burden of administration. Each approach entails a different risk-reward calculus. Full ownership requires legal diligence, rights management, and active engagement with rights organisations. Fractional ownership is more accessible but offers less governance control and typically lower margins.

In sum, understanding royalty structures is not merely a clerical exercise—it is a strategic imperative. Mechanical royalties offer digital regularity but are bound to shifting regulation. Performance royalties offer cultural durability but face latency and macroeconomic exposure. Sync royalties offer spectacular upside but are rare and unpredictable. Only by dissecting the anatomy of these income streams—by examining who pays, when they pay, and why they pay—can investors make informed decisions. Music may move the heart, but if you're putting capital to work in this space, your head must come first.

Case Studies in Cultural Capital

Some assets are priced in spreadsheets; others, in sentiment. When investors acquire intellectual property—particularly music or literary rights—they are not simply purchasing a projected cash flow. They are acquiring a piece of culture that has embedded itself into the emotional lexicon of millions. The financial power of such assets rests not just in their monetisation mechanics, but in their *cultural durability*. The ability of a song or a book to remain meaningful across generations—to resurface in films, be quoted in speeches, or trigger memories in the minds of millions—is what underpins its economic longevity. This chapter examines a series of landmark deals and enduring works to illuminate how cultural capital converts into financial capital, and why the savvy investor must pay as much attention to symbolic relevance as to revenue multiples.

Begin with one of the most talked-about transactions in recent memory: Bob Dylan's sale of his songwriting catalogue to Universal Music Publishing Group in 2020. The reported $300 million price tag stunned many outside the industry. But for insiders, the deal was logical. Dylan's catalogue—spanning over 600 songs—is not just a prolific body of work; it is a cornerstone of 20th-century political, poetic, and social discourse. Songs like "Blowin' in the Wind" and "The Times They Are A-Changin'" have become civil rights anthems, played in classrooms, documentaries, and protests alike. From a valuation standpoint, these tracks generate consistent performance royalties globally and are frequently licensed for film, television, and advertising. More importantly, Dylan's music has no expiration date. Its themes—freedom, injustice, introspection—are permanently relevant. Investors buying catalogues of this calibre are not chasing hits; they are acquiring *social infrastructure*.

Contrast this with the 2021 sale of Taylor Swift's master recordings by private equity firm Shamrock Capital, which purchased them from Scooter Braun's Ithaca Holdings. While Swift did not authorise the sale and subsequently re-recorded her albums, the original masters still hold significant value due to their extensive streaming presence and historical popularity. However, unlike Dylan's catalogue, Swift's early works are tied more to fan identity and commercial pop cycles. They may produce high income now but will be tested over time in terms of cultural endurance. This case illustrates a core tension for investors: *commercial velocity versus emotional permanence*. A catalogue rich in short-term streaming royalties is not inherently superior to one whose songs are used less frequently but across more time-stable contexts—such as Christmas music, wedding staples, or school curricula.

In literature, the same logic applies. Consider the acquisition of Ian Fleming's literary estate—most notably, the James Bond novels. After Fleming's death, his estate retained ownership of his books and subsequently struck deals with publishers, film producers, and merchandising firms. The resulting income stream is multifaceted: print sales, digital licensing, film royalties, and brand tie-ins. Bond, as a character, has outlived Fleming by six decades and remains a household name. Here, the key factor is *narrative universality*. Bond represents archetypes—charm, espionage, masculinity, danger—that remain perennially bankable. Investors looking at literary rights must not merely consider current readership, but ask: *does this intellectual property possess brand elasticity?* Can it evolve across media platforms, international markets, and generational tastes?

A striking example of how cultural resonance creates unforeseen upside is Kate Bush's 1985 song "Running Up That Hill." For decades, it was a niche favourite with a loyal fan base but limited global airplay. Then in 2022, the song featured prominently in the Netflix series Stranger Things, resulting in a streaming explosion and millions in royalties. Bush's royalty agreements reportedly allowed her to retain a substantial portion of this unexpected windfall. The investor lesson here is both cautionary and opportunistic: *the value of a cultural asset is not always visible on a spreadsheet.* Legacy catalogues often contain sleeper hits—works whose time has not yet come, but whose reactivation in a cultural moment can produce outsize returns.

Cultural capital also extends to the moral or ideological dimension of the asset. Nina Simone's music, for instance, has become increasingly licensed in political documentaries, educational programmes, and social justice initiatives. Her estate has witnessed a posthumous surge in sync requests and performance royalties, not because the songs were remixed or rebranded, but because the cultural climate has shifted to re-embrace her voice. In the current climate, owning rights to politically or socially relevant works offers not only financial upside but also reputational positioning. This is particularly relevant for institutional investors or family offices who see intellectual property as part of a broader ESG strategy.

On the publishing side, the acquisition of Roald Dahl's literary catalogue by Netflix illustrates how book rights are being reimagined as intellectual franchises. The reported $686 million acquisition gave Netflix access to the entire Dahl library, with plans to create films, series, and merchandising around his characters. This reflects a broader truth: *the future value of cultural IP increasingly lies in its cross-platform adaptability*. A book, song, or character that can migrate across media—print, screen, stage, audio—multiplies its potential income streams. Investors must therefore consider not just past performance, but *future adaptability* when evaluating cultural assets.

But not all bets pay off. The acquisition of a high-profile catalogue is not a guarantee of future income if the cultural tide turns. Songs tied to now-disgraced celebrities may be blacklisted. Books once considered harmless may be viewed as problematic. These are not theoretical risks—they are real events that have caused catalogue values to plummet. The due diligence process, therefore, must extend beyond financials. It must include reputational audits, audience sentiment analyses, and horizon scanning for potential cultural shifts. A culturally resonant asset can be a gold mine—or a landmine.

Lastly, one must consider the role of custodianship. Unlike owning a stock or bond, owning cultural IP places the investor in a quasi-curatorial position. Decisions about licensing, remastering, or reissuing works carry aesthetic and ethical weight. Mismanagement can alienate audiences or dilute brand equity. Wise investors often partner with experienced creative rights managers who understand not just contracts and cash flow, but tone, timing, and taste. It is this triangulation—between art, audience, and administration—that defines the long-term value of cultural assets.

Cultural capital is not an abstraction. It has form, function, and, critically, *compounding power*. As cultural works age, they either deepen in resonance or fade from memory. The investor's challenge is to identify which assets are merely familiar and which are foundational—works that people return to not because of algorithms, but because they mean something. In that difference lies the entire calculus of sustainable returns.

Chapter 5
Timekeepers of Value—Vintage Watches and Emotional Assets

To the casual observer, a watch might seem merely utilitarian—a device to track hours and minutes. Yet to the discerning collector, investor, or historian, it is far more: a tangible manifestation of legacy, craft, and memory. A vintage timepiece is not simply gears and hands; it is a coded artefact, revealing the confidence of its era, the philosophy of its maker, and the aspirations of its owner. Each watch functions as a portable monument to precision, worn not solely for practicality but as a statement of continuity in an otherwise fragmented world. In today's global asset marketplace—where digital ephemera compete for both attention and capital—vintage watches offer something strikingly different: permanence, materially grounded yet imbued with emotional resonance.

Particularly those from esteemed houses such as Patek Philippe, Rolex, Audemars Piguet, and Omega have evolved from luxury adornments into recognised stores of value. Auction results routinely register six- and seven-figure hammer prices for rare or historically significant pieces. Yet what drives this dramatic appreciation? Why do certain references surge in value while others stagnate? And why do some models attain iconic status seemingly overnight—appearing on celebrity wrists, gracing magazine covers, and igniting fervent demand, all without a change to their mechanical substance?

The explanation is multilayered, sitting at the confluence of engineering, narrative, and identity. This chapter begins by unpacking the criteria for investability: materials, brand, movement architecture, production rarity, provenance, and evolving collector tastes all play their part. Unlike many asset classes, watches are heavily narrative-driven. A piece worn during a moon landing or gifted to a prominent statesman carries an embedded story that tangibly enhances its market value. This is not mere anecdote—it is a measurable multiplier of price.

Yet a modern bifurcation exists: the collector versus the flipper. One operates with patience, research, and reverence for heritage; the other seeks speed, hype, and arbitrage. Each approach carries distinct logic, risk, and reward. Social media, waiting-list scarcity, and grey market dynamics have created layers of speculative froth that can be as lucrative as they are precarious. For an informed investor, understanding these behavioural patterns is crucial. Investing without discerning cult value from intrinsic value is akin to purchasing art without grasping the artist's significance.

Underlying market dynamics is nostalgia, a more subtle but enduring force. Watches are entwined with personal and generational memory—a grandfather's gift, a graduation present, or a model worn by a celebrated athlete or actor. These associations imbue timepieces with psychological heft, driving demand not through cold calculation but through emotional retrieval. When a model resurfaces in cultural consciousness—say the Omega Speedmaster in a space documentary or the Rolex Submariner in a Bond revival—the market reacts. Buyers are not necessarily chasing innovation; they are chasing time itself—or the version they wish to preserve.

Counterfeiting and misinformation, however, have grown in step with rising values. Today's replicas are sophisticated, sometimes requiring microscopic scrutiny and specialised knowledge to detect. Authentication has become a discipline, combining horological expertise, forensic documentation, and provenance verification. Navigating this landscape demands that investors become diligent researchers. This chapter provides cautionary tales and practical guidance: how to vet dealers, interpret serial numbers, and verify service histories.

The rise of watch funds, fractional ownership platforms, and international auction houses demonstrates that watches are now embedded in portfolio theory. They are benchmarked and measured, yet their returns are never purely financial—they carry psychological, reputational, and philosophical dimensions. Ownership communicates taste, patience, and permanence. It compels care and reflection, asking the investor not just to time markets but to engage with time itself: its cycles, its stories, its meaning.

Throughout this chapter, we explore the economic mechanisms and cultural psychology that render vintage watches among the most symbolically and materially rich asset classes available today. We meet those who have built empires from steel and gold, alongside those who have been undone by fads and forgeries. We analyse what distinguishes enduring horological significance from fleeting market noise. And ultimately, we challenge the reader to reconsider how value is stored, transmitted, and worn—one tick at a time.

This is not a guide to next month's must-have watch. It is a meditation on why watches matter, and how they endure as measures of time and vessels of value, long after their original function has become commonplace.

Ticking Assets: What Makes a Watch Investable

There is a reason why, in the hyper-digital world of algorithmic trading and virtual currencies, collectors and investors continue to obsess over small, mechanical instruments worn on the wrist. The investable watch is not merely a measure of time; it is a dense artefact of craftsmanship, brand mythology, and cultural nostalgia. While thousands of models are released every year, only a minute fraction ever cross the invisible threshold from functional accessory to investment-grade asset. What distinguishes them? To answer this question properly is to unpack the layered interplay between engineering, provenance, brand psychology, and market dynamics.

The first and most immediate variable is mechanical integrity. Unlike digital gadgets, which are destined for obsolescence within a few short product cycles, luxury mechanical watches are engineered for longevity—often centuries. A Rolex Submariner or Patek Philippe Calatrava is not simply accurate; it is resilient, serviceable, and constructed from components that resist entropy. The complication count, movement architecture, and finishing details all feed into an undercurrent of perceived permanence. A manual tourbillon by A. Lange & Söhne or a chiming minute repeater from Audemars Piguet doesn't just tell time—it announces a feat of microengineering that rivals aerospace design in complexity. *It is this irreducible craftsmanship that forms the bedrock of long-term value appreciation.*

But mechanics alone are insufficient. A technically brilliant watch that lacks narrative rarely ascends the collector's ladder. Historical context is often the decisive differentiator. The Omega Speedmaster's ascent to investment icon status owes as much to its role in NASA's Apollo programme as it does to its construction. Likewise, Paul Newman's personal Rolex Daytona—a reference once slow to sell at retail—fetched over $17 million at auction not solely due to its condition, but because of its biographical association. The lesson here is fundamental: *provenance can eclipse specifications.* An otherwise ordinary watch becomes exceptional when it is touched by history, or better yet, worn into it.

Brand equity functions as both a gateway and a ceiling. For first-time collectors or investors, names like Rolex, Patek Philippe, and Audemars Piguet offer a sense of reputational safety. These brands have cultivated scarcity, consistency, and legacy over decades—sometimes centuries—and as a result, their watches enjoy high liquidity and resilient second-hand demand. Yet brand alone is no guarantee. Several high-end manufacturers suffer from market fatigue due to overproduction, inconsistent innovation, or reputational drift. Investors must ask not just who made the watch, but when, why, and in what context it was released. *Understanding the cultural moment of a watch's debut is as critical as understanding its movement.*

Scarcity drives demand—but it must be authentic, not manufactured. Limited editions have become a marketing trope across the industry, and many such releases saturate quickly. What separates artificially constrained releases from truly investable pieces is organic scarcity: watches that were produced in low numbers *before* the market deemed them valuable. The 1970s-era Patek Nautilus 3700, once a commercial underperformer, now commands six-figure valuations because few examples were made and even fewer were preserved in original condition. The market punishes contrivance but rewards patience. *True scarcity is discovered retrospectively, not proclaimed on a box.*

Condition, naturally, remains a pillar of valuation, but here the rules diverge from those governing other collectibles. With vintage watches, 'perfect' does not always mean mint. Collectors may prize a faded bezel or tropical dial for its aesthetic patina and uniqueness. An untouched, all-original Rolex GMT-Master with slight weathering may be worth significantly more than a later serviced model with replaced parts, even if the latter is in technically better shape. This nuance reflects a deep principle in watch collecting: *authentic wear is proof of life, not damage.* The goal is to identify integrity, not to erase history.

Market perception can often deviate from collector wisdom, especially in moments of economic flux. Short-term investors may chase models that are 'hot' on Instagram, driving price spikes for watches that lack historical legs. The 2021 bull run in stainless steel sports watches—fueled by celebrity endorsements and artificial scarcity—saw massive premiums on models like the Audemars Piguet Royal Oak and Rolex Daytona. By mid-2023, many of those same watches corrected by 20–40% as liquidity pressures returned. Here lies a sobering truth: *hype is a cycle; heritage is a trajectory.* The investor who learns to tell the difference does not simply follow the market—they anticipate it.

One of the more overlooked variables is regional taste. Watch desirability is not a monolith. A model celebrated in Geneva may languish in Tokyo. A dial colour prized in the Middle East might underperform in North America. These cultural asymmetries, while subtle, create arbitrage opportunities for the geographically aware investor. For example, the Cartier Crash—long a cult favourite in London—only recently gained traction in the U.S. market, driving a sharp uptick in demand and auction prices. *Understanding regional sentiment is an undervalued skill in an increasingly globalised secondary market.*

Even the most seasoned investors can fall prey to tunnel vision. The dominance of a few flagship models—such as the Rolex Submariner, Patek Philippe Nautilus, or Audemars Piguet Royal Oak—can obscure emerging categories with meaningful upside. Independent brands like F.P. Journe, Laurent Ferrier, or Rexhep Rexhepi have cultivated loyal, educated followings that now rival the major houses in value appreciation. The collector who studies craftsmanship, not just commercial buzz, is often first to discover these undervalued opportunities. *Watch investment is as much a connoisseur's sport as it is a financial discipline.*

There is also a philosophical dimension to consider. A vintage watch is one of the few assets that offers enjoyment, display, and inheritance while quietly appreciating in value. Unlike equities or property, a well-chosen timepiece can be worn, admired, and passed on with a minimum of friction or dilution. It is not merely a vehicle for wealth storage, but a statement of taste, patience, and custodianship. *The best watches are not just held—they are lived with, and through.* This blurring of function and emotion adds a layer of meaning that few other assets can match.

Yet precisely because watches straddle the aesthetic and economic realms, they require a hybrid intelligence to evaluate properly. An investor must be as attuned to brand messaging as they are to balance sheets; as aware of auction trends as they are of horological milestones. Without such nuance, one risks conflating collectibility with durability, or scarcity with significance. The margin for error can be thin, and the cost of misjudgement real.

What makes a watch investable, then, is not a formula—it is a symphony of converging signals. Movement, provenance, brand integrity, design, scarcity, condition, market awareness, and emotional resonance all contribute in varying degrees. But above all, it is the investor's *discernment*—their ability to distinguish signal from noise, heritage from hype—that transforms a watch from a fashion statement into an appreciating asset. Watches may tick, but value accumulates in silence.

Collectors vs. Flippers: Two Mindsets, Two Outcomes

The vintage watch market is not merely a reflection of supply and demand—it is a psychological arena where time preference, status sensitivity, and emotional attachment battle for dominance. At the heart of this arena stand two archetypes with diametrically opposed orientations: the collector and the flipper. Their motivations, time horizons, risk appetites, and cognitive frames diverge so significantly that, although they may handle the same objects, they are playing entirely different games. Understanding the distinction between these mindsets is not a trivial exercise in typology. It reveals the very mechanics of market cycles, pricing distortions, and long-term valuation trends in the luxury timepiece ecosystem.

The collector is driven by connoisseurship. This is not to say they are immune to financial return—many collectors have built enormous wealth through their portfolios—but their primary currency is meaning. A collector buys with intent and holds with conviction. Every acquisition must justify its place in a narrative that is intellectual as much as aesthetic: a lineage of brands, eras, movements, materials, or milestones that reflect a personal or historical logic. The watch is not merely possessed; it is understood. The collector is acutely aware of the movement inside the case, the evolution of the reference number, the significance of the dial variant, and even the socio-cultural context of the original release. For them, *value is accreted through knowledge, not momentum.*

Contrast this with the flipper, whose orientation is toward momentum and opportunity. The flipper thrives on inefficiencies in the short-term market—leveraging scarcity, hype, or regional mispricings to extract quick profit. Their holding period is often counted in weeks or months, not years. They prioritise liquidity over legacy, packaging rather than provenance. Where the collector analyses factory records, the flipper tracks Discord chats. One is building a library; the other is running a trading desk. This is not necessarily a condemnation. Flippers serve a function in the ecosystem by injecting liquidity and price discovery. But *their incentives are inherently destabilising to long-term value creation.*

To an outsider, both groups may appear to be simply buying and selling watches. Yet the underlying motivations are more than economic—they are philosophical. The collector sees a watch as a vessel of memory and craft; the flipper sees it as a tradeable commodity. This bifurcation leads to different behaviours during downturns. In soft markets, collectors tend to hold or even acquire selectively, guided by conviction in the intrinsic worth of what they own. Flippers, by contrast, exit quickly, often creating downward pressure on prices as they offload inventory. *The collector is playing a game of permanence; the flipper, of velocity.*

The psychology behind each profile can be traced to deeper cognitive biases. Collectors are often afflicted by the endowment effect—the tendency to overvalue objects one owns due to the emotional investment attached to them. Their watches become extensions of identity, making them reluctant to part with even appreciating assets. Flippers, on the other hand, are more vulnerable to recency bias and herd dynamics. They follow trends, chase spikes, and often make purchases based on what is hot rather than what is historically significant. These behaviours are not just academic distinctions—they shape the volatility and price elasticity of the market itself.

A clear illustration of this divergence came during the pandemic-era bull market. As waiting lists ballooned and supply chains stalled, flippers drove prices of steel sports models—particularly Rolex, Patek Philippe, and Audemars Piguet—to unprecedented highs. Many of these watches doubled or tripled in price on the grey market within months of release. Flippers fuelled this rise by pre-ordering multiple units, often using connections at authorised dealers or paying premiums for immediate delivery. Collectors watched cautiously, recognising the inflation as unsustainable. When macroeconomic pressures and monetary tightening hit in 2022–2023, the correction was swift. Watches that had been flipped at a premium were suddenly trading below retail. Those who had bought on hype were left holding assets with no emotional anchor—mere metal. *The collector is insulated by conviction; the flipper is exposed by sentiment.*

This dynamic plays out across other asset classes but is uniquely amplified in the watch world because of the emotional weight these objects carry. A watch is not like a stock or bond. It can be worn, admired, inherited. It has presence. The collector respects this alchemy. The flipper, if successful, monetises it. But there is an inherent tension: *the more a market becomes dominated by flippers, the less authentic it becomes for collectors—and vice versa.*

What makes this tension particularly complex is that many market participants evolve from one role to the other. A young flipper may stumble into collecting after realising that certain pieces—those with personal resonance or horological uniqueness—are worth keeping. Conversely, some collectors, driven by rising values and peer influence, begin to speculate, rationalising short-term trades under the guise of "portfolio management." The boundary is porous, but the distinction in mindset remains stark. The key difference is intent: *is the goal to preserve or to extract?*

This divide has strategic implications for investors considering entry into the vintage watch market. If your orientation is primarily financial, adopting a collector's depth of knowledge can mitigate the risks associated with speculative buying. Understanding the nuances of dial variants, reference evolutions, and auction history will offer stronger price resilience than following social media trends. Likewise, if you are an emotional buyer, awareness of flipper dynamics can inoculate you against overpaying during hype cycles. Every investor, regardless of profile, benefits from recognising when they are being influenced by the opposite camp.

It's worth noting that brands themselves are increasingly aware of these dynamics. Companies like Rolex and Audemars Piguet have launched certified pre-owned programmes to counteract grey market volatility and reclaim control over pricing. Others, like Patek Philippe, have openly discouraged flipping by restricting allocations and tracking resale behaviour. These are not merely commercial manoeuvres; they are efforts to realign the market with long-term collectors rather than short-term arbitrageurs. *The industry knows that lasting value is built not on hype, but on heritage.*

As with all collectables, watches exist in a liminal space between utility and narrative. The collector preserves that narrative. The flipper exploits its momentary exaggerations. But it is the tension between these two mindsets that makes the market both volatile and vibrant. *One sees time as a canvas; the other as a clock.*

The implication for the thoughtful investor is clear: you must know which game you are playing. There is no shame in flipping, and no sanctimony in collecting. But confusing the two is dangerous. A watch bought as a speculative play should not be mistaken for a store of legacy. Likewise, a grail piece chosen for its historical significance should not be rushed to resale because of market noise. *Clarity of intent is the first discipline of watch investing.*

Understanding this psychological and behavioural split is not a footnote in the story of horological assets—it is the lens through which every transaction must be interpreted. When you recognise whether you are dealing with a collector or a flipper, you do not simply see who they are—you begin to see where the market is heading.

Market Moments and Temporal Myths

The most powerful force in the vintage watch market is not precision engineering or brand marketing. It is memory. More precisely, *shared memory filtered through time and scarcity, myth and emotion.* While mechanical complexity and provenance provide the scaffolding for a timepiece's valuation, it is nostalgia—deep, generational, often irrational—that inflates the market's most iconic moments. An investment in vintage watches, then, is not just a bet on tangible craftsmanship but on the persistence of cultural memory. Understanding how this dynamic operates—how timepieces become vessels for longing and social significance—is critical to reading the market's irrational peaks and durable premiums.

No brand has capitalised on this mythology better than Rolex. Consider the Paul Newman Daytona. When it first appeared in the 1960s, it was a commercial failure. Dealers struggled to move them. Today, those same models sell for hundreds of thousands—sometimes millions—of dollars. The transformation was not driven by horological breakthroughs but by cultural association. Paul Newman's personal style, immortalised through photographs and racing heritage, elevated an unpopular variant into a grail object. The story added texture; the scarcity did the rest. *This is the blueprint for temporal myth-making: historical insignificance upgraded by retrospective emotional value.*

Scarcity alone, however, does not suffice. The market is awash in rare pieces that command little attention. What distinguishes investable scarcity is recognisability. Collectors pay premiums not merely for limited production runs but for *shared knowledge of those limits.* A rare watch unknown to the community might remain undervalued for decades; a moderately rare one featured on a celebrity's wrist or in a prestige auction catalogue can triple in value in a matter of weeks. *Scarcity must be visible to activate demand.* This visibility is often shaped not by the brand, but by community storytelling—watch forums, collector meetups, editorial profiles, and social media echo chambers.

The generational element adds another layer of complexity. What boomers once regarded as tool watches—Omega Speedmasters, Heuer Carreras—millennials now covet as luxury relics of industrial-era masculinity. This is not merely a function of design preference.

It is a longing for perceived authenticity, an antidote to the disposable minimalism of the digital age. As younger collectors enter the market, they reach backward—not because those watches are objectively superior, but because *they encode values now seen as scarce: permanence, manual craftsmanship, analogue charm.* This is particularly evident in the resurgence of interest in 1970s integrated bracelet sports watches. Their appeal today is less about utility and more about their reflection of a bygone design confidence.

These generational shifts create identifiable market moments. When Phillips Auction sold Paul Newman's personal Daytona for $17.8 million in 2017, it didn't just set a record—it catalysed a wave of interest in vintage chronographs more broadly. Lesser-known variants saw prices spike. Watch media outlets declared a new golden age of collecting. Investors who understood the power of the moment capitalised. Those who dismissed it as irrational missed an important truth: *in markets tied to cultural capital, irrationality can be persistent and profitable.*

Manufacturers have grown acutely aware of this psychological lever. Omega's "Speedy Tuesday" releases and TAG Heuer's reissues of vintage Carreras are not nostalgic by accident. They are strategic manipulations of emotional memory, calibrated for audiences who crave historical resonance with modern execution. These reissues blur the line between past and present, creating *synthetic nostalgia*—an engineered sense of having missed something valuable that is now being re-offered, but in limited numbers. This creates urgency. It also complicates valuation: are you buying heritage, or the illusion of it?

Market participants must also reckon with the difference between *authentic nostalgia and cyclical trend.* The former is grounded in lived or inherited experience; the latter in aesthetic recycling. The interest in 1980s digital Casio models, for example, reflects a legitimate resurgence of childhood memory for Gen X and older millennials. By contrast, the hype around rainbow-bezel Rolexes or iced-out APs is trend-driven, often disconnected from historical significance. *Only one of these categories has shown long-term price resilience.*

A striking example of cyclical myth creation is the Patek Philippe Nautilus 5711. For years, it was respected but not revered. Then came an avalanche of media profiles, celebrity endorsements, and secondary market scarcity. When Patek announced its discontinuation, values soared to irrational highs. But unlike the Paul Newman Daytona, the 5711 lacked a foundational myth. It became a status object too quickly, without the sediment of collector lore to stabilise its significance. When prices eventually corrected, it revealed a crucial insight: *the speed of hype inversely correlates with the durability of premium.* Fast mythologies fade. Durable ones accrete slowly.

Understanding these dynamics equips the serious investor with a set of interpretive tools. Rather than chasing models at their media peak, watch investors would do well to study those pieces quietly gaining cultural weight. A watch worn by a significant figure in an under-documented era, or a reference quietly revered by expert collectors but ignored by lifestyle magazines, often presents better upside than the headline piece of the season. *Myths are most valuable before they become obvious.*

There is also an ethical dimension worth surfacing. When market actors exploit nostalgia without respecting its roots—when flippers hoard limited releases to generate artificial scarcity—they undermine the very trust that sustains long-term collectability. Much like the art market, the value of a vintage watch is not just its materials or mechanics but the *integrity of the community that validates it.* If trust collapses, so too does the premium. Investors and collectors alike must be mindful that *the myth is only as powerful as the belief that sustains it.*

Ultimately, to understand why one watch commands a 10x premium over another despite similar materials and movement is to understand the currency of collective memory. A watch is a physical object, yes—but it is also an emotional timestamp. It marks not just hours and minutes, but cultural moments, personal milestones, aesthetic revolutions. The market assigns value not only to what a watch does, but to *what it reminds us of.* And as long as human memory continues to privilege certain periods, people, and design cues over others, there will always be asymmetric opportunities for those who understand how myths inflate—and sometimes define—markets.

Verifying Time: Avoiding Counterfeits and Market Hype

The very qualities that make vintage watches desirable—craftsmanship, scarcity, and historical prestige—are the same traits that make them ideal targets for counterfeiting and speculative manipulation. In a market where an added patina can mean an added zero to a price tag, due diligence is no longer optional. It is foundational. The assumption that a vintage watch's worth is self-evident is a costly error. *Authenticity is no longer a matter of visual inspection alone; it demands forensic attention, contextual knowledge, and a sceptical mind.*

High-end counterfeits have become so advanced that even seasoned collectors have been fooled. The era of cartoonishly fake Rolexes with ticking second hands is over. Today, forgeries may include hand-aged lume, period-correct fonts, and repurposed vintage parts. Some are built using original movements but recased in skilfully manipulated housings. Others are "Frankenwatches," amalgamations of legitimate components from various models assembled into something that mimics a high-value reference. *These hybrids are the most dangerous because they are not outright fakes; they are historical distortions.*

Consider the infamous "Cartier Crash" incident, in which several supposedly rare models entered the secondary market in rapid succession, raising eyebrows among collectors. Subsequent investigations revealed inconsistencies in hallmarks and production chronology. But by that point, transactions had occurred, reputations had been risked, and the price benchmark had been manipulated. *The damage in the vintage market is often reputational before it is financial—and recovery is slow and uneven.*

Serious investors must begin with documentation. Provenance, when available, is invaluable. Original purchase receipts, service records, warranty papers, and even period photographs of the watch in use form a chain of custody that dramatically reduces the risk of counterfeit. But documentation can be forged as well. Thus, authenticity verification should extend to serial number tracing and caseback inspection, ideally by a recognised brand-authorised watchmaker or auction house specialist. *The goal is triangulation: overlapping sources of truth that reduce the margin of deception.*

Inspection of patina is another key point of investigation. The way a dial ages—its coloration, spotting, or fading—should align with the known behaviour of materials from that era. Radium lume from the 1940s behaves differently than tritium from the 1960s. If a watch appears too pristine for its age or if the degradation seems inconsistent with material science, it warrants scrutiny. Artificial patination techniques exist and can fool even the trained eye. UV light testing, chemical residue analysis, and dial paint dating are tools increasingly employed in high-value verifications. *Anomalies are not always evidence of fraud—but they demand explanation before investment.*

Market hype represents a more insidious form of distortion. While counterfeits are tangible deceptions, hype inflates value on the basis of *emotional momentum rather than fundamentals*. Limited releases and brand-engineered scarcity often create false urgency. The 2021 Patek Philippe Nautilus "Tiffany Blue" collaboration is a textbook case: a 5711 variant with aesthetic novelty, released in constrained quantities, saw prices skyrocket overnight. But the question for investors is not "Will it rise?" but "Will it *sustain*?" *Markets built on narrative rather than substance tend to correct abruptly and mercilessly.*

Social media amplifies hype dynamics to dangerous levels. A celebrity wristshot or YouTube unboxing can turn an obscure reference into a must-have grail in days. This dynamic flattens discernment: context is stripped away, replaced by dopamine-fuelled mimicry. For watch investors, the key is to resist the false clarity of consensus. A surge in popularity does not imply long-term investability. *Ask what historical context underpins the demand—and who stands to benefit from the spike.*

Auction houses play a paradoxical role. On one hand, they provide authentication, price discovery, and institutional legitimacy. On the other, they are commercial enterprises that benefit from inflated valuations. While reputable houses like Phillips or Christie's maintain rigorous vetting standards, the growing pressure to deliver record sales introduces perverse incentives. Restored watches may be marketed as "original condition," provenance may be stretched, and catalogue descriptions may elide caveats. *Investors must read not only the lot description but the omissions within it.*

An often-overlooked risk in vintage watch collecting is over-restoration. A watch that has been "too carefully" serviced—new dial, polished case, aftermarket parts—may function better but is usually worth less. Collectors pay for originality, even if it includes cosmetic imperfection. The best-preserved timepieces show wear that is consistent, honest, and irreplicable. Service replacement parts, even from the original manufacturer, often dilute historical value. *An untouched vintage Submariner with a cracked acrylic crystal may be worth more than a "refreshed" version with all factory-new components.*

There is also the challenge of interpreting catalogue nomenclature. Terms like "tropical dial," "ghost bezel," or "pre-Moon" are now deployed as value-enhancing descriptors, but their definitions are often elastic. A dial with heat-induced discolouration may be romanticised as "tropical" even if the effect is environmental degradation rather than design feature. The absence of clear industry standards allows for creative reinterpretation of defects as charm. *Knowing the distinction between marketable myth and material truth is critical to making sound decisions.*

Digital marketplaces have widened access but introduced new vectors of risk. Platforms like Chrono24, WatchBox, and eBay offer global reach, but quality control varies. Verified dealer badges are useful but not infallible. Escrow services help, but post-sale support is inconsistent. Here, the investor must apply the same caution they would to any other financial instrument: *If you would not buy a stock without audited financials, do not buy a watch without comprehensive documentation and expert verification.*

Education is the ultimate safeguard. The more an investor understands reference numbers, dial variants, model timelines, and manufacturing idiosyncrasies, the less likely they are to be misled. But education is slow, and the market is fast. For this reason, forming relationships with trusted experts—dealers, horologists, restoration specialists—is indispensable. Reputation in this space is not just currency; it is insurance. *Knowing whom to trust is as important as knowing what to buy.*

Vintage watches, at their best, offer a unique blend of financial potential and historical beauty. But the romance of timekeeping must be grounded in forensic reality. The market does not reward naivety. It rewards rigour, scepticism, and discernment. In a space where a single numeral on a caseback can separate a $5,000 watch from a $50,000 one, details are not pedantic—they are decisive. Authenticating a watch is not simply about avoiding fraud. It is about protecting the integrity of one's investment and preserving the historical fidelity of the object itself. And that, ultimately, is the investor's highest responsibility: not just to own a piece of time, but to verify that it is truly what it claims to be.

Chapter 6
Liquid Rarity—Wine, Art, and the Language of Taste

The relationship between taste and value has never been straightforward, and in contemporary investing, it grows ever more intricate—and consequential. Wine and art, once the quiet indulgences of a cultured few, have evolved into instruments of financial strategy that are dynamic, opaque, and often unpredictable. These markets exist at the margins, where scarcity intersects with narrative, and where pricing is less a reflection of measurable output than of collective belief. Unlike stocks or bonds, their worth cannot be captured solely by decimals or discounted cash flows. Value resides in perception, provenance, and the shifting preferences of generations inheriting both capital and culture. This chapter examines how wine and art—two of humanity's oldest repositories of taste—are now being repurposed as vehicles for wealth preservation, diversification, and speculative opportunity.

To engage with wine and art as asset classes requires a different mindset. These are not yield-bearing instruments in the conventional sense, nor are they passive holdings. They do not conform to the efficient-market assumptions underpinning equities or bonds. Instead, they occupy a space where emotion and expertise converge. A 1982 Château Lafite Rothschild or a Jean-Michel Basquiat canvas is not merely a commodity—it is a signal. Ownership signals access, discernment, conviction, and positioning. Investing in these assets entails entering a market whose currency includes cultural literacy, curatorial skill, and a tolerance for ambiguity. There is no quarterly report for a Damien Hirst installation, no P/E ratio for a magnum of Domaine de la Romanée-Conti. Yet these objects command prices that routinely confound traditional notions of rational valuation—until one examines demand in context.

Wine, in particular, is frequently misunderstood as an investment. Its maturation, consumption, and valuation are influenced by a host of factors, both geological and geopolitical. Climatic anomalies can alter vineyard outputs; trade policies can shift distribution; critical acclaim from a single reviewer can dramatically affect market interest. Above all, wine is finite: bottles are opened, corks deteriorate, and storage conditions vary. For the knowledgeable investor, scarcity is tangible. The longer a properly cellared vintage remains intact, the rarer it becomes—not theoretically, but in absolute global volume.

Yet scarcity alone is insufficient without rigorous attention to provenance and condition. Authenticity depends on more than label verification: temperature-controlled storage, meticulous documentation, and unbroken chain of custody are paramount. The fine wine market has responded with institutional infrastructure: bonded warehouses, insurance-backed custodianship, and regulated trading platforms such as Liv-ex provide liquidity without necessitating the physical movement of assets. Storage is not overhead; it is foundational. Neglect it, and value erodes.

Art presents a distinct challenge: interpretation. Unlike wine, which is shaped by soil and climate, art is shaped by semiotics, context, and perception. A work may be critically acclaimed yet commercially inert; another, deemed derivative, may command astronomical prices at auction. Understanding appreciation requires engaging with the ecosystem surrounding creation: museums, gallerists, critics, auction houses, and increasingly, algorithms. The opacity of the art market is deliberate, selectively rewarding those fluent in its internal language.

Curation often drives art's market performance as much as creation. A painting's presence in a major retrospective, inclusion in a catalogue raisonné, or exhibition history across institutions can elevate its standing. Conversely, a work remaining in private hands without record may struggle to realise its full potential. In art, visibility is provenance: a strategic placement can materially affect value. Collectors who navigate this subtle politics—loaning to museums, aligning with influential dealers—often achieve superior returns when liquidity becomes the objective.

In both wine and art, taste transforms from preference into strategy. Developing a palate requires time, exposure, and mentorship. It is not about following critics or trends blindly, but understanding how value is constructed within cultural frameworks that shift across geography and generations. A Hong Kong collector may prize vintages differently than a London investor. A millennial buyer in Los Angeles may elevate a digital artist unrecognised by European institutions. Taste is fluid, informed by proximity to both capital and culture.

Participating meaningfully in these markets demands fluency in their grammar. Signals—overt or subtle—shape perception: a vintage's classification, a château's reputation, an artist's representation, an exhibition's timing. Like any language, mastery requires immersion. Serious investors read beyond headlines, discerning how context drives both perceived and realised value.

Subjectivity is unavoidable. Traditional investors seek control, quantifiability, and backtesting. Wine and art deny these comforts. They require tolerance for ambiguity: imperfect price transparency, contingent future value, and situational liquidity. Yet these very traits allow perceptive participants to generate outsized returns. In inefficient markets, edge arises not from speed but from insight—from anticipating shifts in taste and recognising emerging scarcity.

Operationally, these assets introduce unique complexities. Wine demands strict temperature and humidity control, ideally in bonded facilities. Art requires conservation protocols, climate regulation, and comprehensive insurance. Resale is nuanced: secondary wine markets vary by jurisdiction and taxation; art resale may involve royalties, gallery commissions, and unpredictable auction dynamics. Ownership is stewardship. Mismanagement erodes value, legal ambiguity restricts liquidity, and logistical oversights can destroy an otherwise sound investment.

This chapter provides frameworks for assessing investable wine and art, integrating both qualitative sensibilities and quantitative indicators. We explore how prestige is constructed, scarcity discovered or manufactured, and institutions—public and private—shape visibility and valuation. Taste emerges not as a soft skill, but a tactical one, creating a moat against volatility. We also dissect the physical, legal, and logistical infrastructure necessary to manage these investments ethically, effectively, and profitably.

These markets are far from simple, yet they are profoundly human. Engaging with them is to engage with history, beauty, and belief. Wine and art teach us to measure worth not only in numbers, but in narrative. In a financial landscape increasingly dominated by algorithms, such fluency may prove the rarest—and most rewarding—asset of all.

The Palate Portfolio: Investing in Wine

Wine is one of the few consumable luxuries that also behaves like a long-term financial instrument. Unlike stocks or bonds, which exist within an abstract digital economy, fine wine is grounded in the physical world—subject to weather, soil, and time. And yet, it trades on global exchanges, is securitised in institutional portfolios, and is increasingly held not in cellars but in bonded warehouses, awaiting future liquidity events. Wine occupies a rare space in the investment universe: part indulgence, part artefact, part alternative asset. But what transforms a bottle into a bankable instrument? The answer lies in a precise combination of terroir, provenance, scarcity, and a sophisticated global market machinery that prizes both prestige and patience.

To treat wine as an investable asset requires a fundamental shift in mindset. This is not about preference or palate. It is about predictability, pedigree, and preservation. The moment wine is no longer purchased to be poured but to be held, its financial life begins. That transition—from consumable to collectible—demands a rigorous understanding of the mechanics that underlie its valuation, ageing potential, and resale ecosystem.

The foundation of wine's financial appeal is its *ageing potential.* Unlike most commodities, high-end wines often improve with time. Their chemical structure evolves in the bottle, enhancing aroma, flavour complexity, and mouthfeel. This alchemy of time adds not only taste but value. Yet, ageing is not uniform across all wines. Bordeaux's Left Bank reds, certain Burgundies, Barolos, and Napa Valley Cabernets have reputations for developing over decades, while others may peak within five to seven years. The difference between a wine that improves with time and one that deteriorates is the difference between an appreciating asset and a depreciating good. Investors must therefore cultivate fluency in *vinous lifecycles*—understanding how climate, vintage conditions, varietals, and winemaking techniques affect maturation trajectories.

Closely tied to ageing is the role of *provenance*. In the wine world, provenance is not mere marketing gloss; it is essential due diligence. Provenance refers to a wine's documented history—from the moment it left the estate to its current storage conditions. The finest wines are acutely sensitive to temperature, light, and vibration. A bottle kept in a temperature-controlled bonded warehouse commands a premium over one that travelled in someone's luggage from a Paris wine shop. The more prestigious the wine, the more scrutiny its journey undergoes. Fraudulent bottlings, especially of sought-after vintages, are not rare. In fact, they're so common that entire businesses now specialise in forensic bottle authentication, complete with cork and glass analysis, ultraviolet label scans, and ownership chain verification. In the investment world, *a flawless bottle with poor provenance is a financial liability*.

The next key element is *global demand cycles*. Wine investment is not just about intrinsic quality—it's also about perception and market appetite. The emergence of Asia, particularly China and Hong Kong, as major fine wine buyers in the early 2000s reshaped the landscape. Château Lafite Rothschild, once a staple of European collections, saw its prices soar as it became a status symbol among Chinese elites. Similar dynamics have unfolded with Super Tuscans in the US or cult Napa Cabernets in the UK. These are not accidental shifts; they reflect a fusion of economic growth, cultural aspiration, and strategic brand marketing. For the investor, understanding these cycles means tracking geopolitical movements, import tariff changes, and even luxury consumption psychology. *Taste, in this context, becomes a global index*.

However, investment viability isn't dictated solely by branding or demand—it also hinges on market infrastructure. In recent decades, wine has become increasingly *financialised.* Platforms such as Liv-ex (the London International Vintners Exchange) have introduced transparency, liquidity, and price discovery mechanisms previously absent in wine trading. Liv-ex provides real-time pricing data, index tracking, and trade execution for thousands of wines globally. This has enabled the creation of wine funds, fractional ownership models, and even NFTs linked to bottles held in professional storage. Institutional investors now allocate portions of their alternative asset budgets to wine, viewing it as a hedge against inflation and equity volatility. Its low correlation to traditional asset classes, combined with historical resilience during downturns, has solidified its place as a *defensive luxury* in portfolios.

Yet, financialisation is a double-edged sword. As wine becomes commodified, there's a temptation to treat it as just another line item—detached from the cultural, environmental, and human factors that shape it. Unlike stocks, a bottle of Domaine de la Romanée-Conti cannot be duplicated or scaled. Its scarcity is intrinsic, not manufactured. Its value, while subject to market forces, is also grounded in heritage, terroir, and craftsmanship. Investors who overlook these intangibles—who reduce wine to charts and indices—risk missing both financial nuance and cultural depth. *True value in wine is never only numerical; it is narrative.*

This is where vintage matters. Not every year produces investable wine, even at the most revered estates. Climatic conditions—late frosts, excessive rainfall, heat spikes—can severely affect quality. A poor vintage will not age well and may underperform even if brand name suggests otherwise. Conversely, a stellar vintage can elevate second-tier producers into prime investment territory. The 2005 and 2010 Bordeaux vintages, for example, saw quality leap across the board, offering profitable entry points beyond First Growth labels. Investors attuned to *vintage analysis*—reading weather reports as closely as yield curves—are better positioned to identify underpriced gems before they ascend into blue-chip status.

Storage is another underappreciated determinant of success. Holding fine wine is not passive. Professional storage, ideally in bonded warehouses, ensures optimal conditions and tax efficiency. Wines stored in bond remain exempt from VAT and duty, preserving margins upon resale. Moreover, documentation from such facilities strengthens provenance, enhancing buyer confidence. Some investors choose to store with major merchants or third-party custodians who specialise in wine as an asset class. This enables better portfolio management, access to broader trading networks, and real-time valuation updates.

The wine investor must also navigate the *liquidity paradox*. While fine wine markets are more accessible than ever, they remain less liquid than equities or REITs. Exit timelines can stretch depending on the vintage, the economic climate, and buyer interest. Auctions (Sotheby's, Christie's), merchant networks, and platforms like Cult Wines or WineBid provide channels—but each involves fees, timing considerations, and buyer volatility. A well-curated wine portfolio is more akin to private equity than public stock—it requires patience, discernment, and often, a medium-to-long horizon.

Critically, ethical considerations are emerging in wine investment. Climate change threatens traditional growing regions—Burgundy, Bordeaux, Napa—and is pushing winemakers to higher altitudes and latitudes. Investors must start asking: how climate-resilient is my wine portfolio? Can a vineyard's success today be sustained tomorrow? Furthermore, cultural shifts are challenging the exclusivity narratives long attached to wine. Younger consumers in emerging markets may prioritise sustainability and transparency over vintage prestige. The investor who ignores these signals risks holding assets that lose cultural relevance even as they retain technical quality.

Ultimately, investing in wine is not about drinking habits but about *interpretive skill.* It demands the ability to read between the layers: between taste and market data, between heritage and hype, between volatility and value. A bottle is never just a bottle—it is geography, history, chemistry, reputation, and belief. When those elements align, it becomes investable. When they diverge, it becomes speculative. *The disciplined wine investor knows the difference.* And it is that discernment, not just capital, that defines long-term returns in this arena.

Why Art Appreciates (and Sometimes Doesn't)

A painting does not appreciate in value because it is beautiful. It appreciates because it is *believed in.* That belief—shared by collectors, institutions, critics, and markets—is what turns canvas and pigment into capital. To invest in visual art is to engage with a system of taste, power, scarcity, and narrative. And yet, many approach the art market armed only with aesthetic instinct, unaware that value in this space is rarely intuitive. The Mona Lisa's financial worth is not due to her smile. Jackson Pollock's drip paintings didn't gain prominence through popularity alone. In the art world, *value is manufactured, maintained, and sometimes manipulated* by forces that lie beyond the frame.

To understand what makes visual art a viable asset class—and why some works appreciate while others stagnate—one must examine the mechanisms of cultural production alongside the machinery of the market. It begins with a fundamental question: *What constitutes value in art?* Unlike equities, which yield cash flow, or property, which generates rental income, art provides no intrinsic economic return. Its value is relational—dependent on what others are willing to pay. This makes the art market uniquely speculative, but not irrational. A deep logic underpins its apparent volatility, and the key to unlocking that logic lies in tracing how artworks are validated, circulated, and ultimately canonised.

At the core of value formation is the *artist's career trajectory*. Early works by artists who later become significant often appreciate dramatically, not because of the object's independent quality, but because the artist's importance has been institutionally validated—through major exhibitions, museum acquisitions, critical discourse, and inclusion in academic canons. This career arc is cultivated by a network of actors: gallerists, curators, critics, collectors, and auction houses. Each plays a role in elevating the artist's market standing. A solo exhibition at MoMA or Tate Modern can catalyse demand, sending prices into seven or eight figures. But these institutional nods are not organic—they are the product of curatorial decisions, reputational networks, and long-term relationship management. *The art market rewards narrative as much as output.*

Art also appreciates when it is seen as culturally or historically pivotal. Consider Jean-Michel Basquiat. In his lifetime, his work was controversial, sometimes dismissed. Today, his pieces regularly command tens of millions of dollars. That appreciation is not merely due to retrospective revaluation of skill; it is due to his repositioning as a foundational figure in postmodern American art, bridging graffiti, neo-expressionism, and Black cultural identity. Similarly, works from female artists previously overlooked—such as Hilma af Klint or Lee Krasner—have seen exponential growth as the art world seeks to redress historic imbalances. *Markets move when narratives shift.*

However, not all aesthetic success translates into financial appreciation. Thousands of skilled, even beloved, artists never break into investment-grade territory. Why? Because art's value is also a function of *scarcity and circulation.* A unique piece by a recognised master, backed by a limited output and an active secondary market, is far more likely to appreciate than widely reproduced or commercially saturated work. For instance, Andy Warhol's silkscreens, despite their mechanical production, are tightly catalogued and meticulously tracked. Their value is sustained by brand coherence and curated scarcity. In contrast, an emerging artist with prolific output but no institutional representation may create beautiful work, but their market remains fragmented, speculative, and vulnerable to dilution.

Crucially, *provenance and authenticity* underpin every significant appreciation curve. The art market has been plagued by forgeries—from Han van Meegeren's fake Vermeers to the Knoedler Gallery scandal in New York, where dozens of counterfeit Abstract Expressionist works were sold to unsuspecting collectors. A solid paper trail—exhibition history, ownership records, certificates of authenticity—is not optional but essential. Buyers at the top end of the market conduct forensic examinations, sometimes involving chemical pigment analysis or x-ray imaging. A single question mark over authenticity can reduce a work's value to zero. *In art, trust is capital.*

Economic context also shapes appreciation. During periods of inflation, tangible assets like art tend to outperform. Ultra-high-net-worth individuals, seeking to hedge against currency devaluation or stock market volatility, increasingly turn to art as a store of value. This "flight to quality" drives demand for blue-chip works by historically validated artists—Picasso, Rothko, Richter—whose markets are seen as relatively stable. Conversely, in recessions or during liquidity crunches, speculative sectors of the market—emerging artists, mid-tier contemporary work—tend to contract sharply. In 2009, following the financial crisis, many younger artists saw prices halve or worse, while the very top of the market remained resilient. *Art appreciation is not evenly distributed—it mirrors the broader wealth structure.*

Another major force shaping value is the role of *auction houses.* Christie's, Sotheby's, and Phillips do not merely reflect the market; they shape it. Their marketing machines, curated sales, and public results contribute to price discovery and artist visibility. A record-breaking auction result can create an upward feedback loop: collectors reassess, galleries reprice, museums take note, and a new ceiling is set. But auctions also reveal vulnerabilities. If a work is passed or sells below estimate, it can tarnish the artist's market. The auction world is high stakes and high visibility—offering both acceleration and exposure. *It is not just where art is sold, but how and when.*

Market manipulation is not unheard of. There are documented instances where galleries or collectors buy works at auction to inflate prices and then cite those prices as benchmarks in private sales. This practice, though legally grey, underscores the fact that *art markets are not perfectly efficient.* They are influenced by insider knowledge, opaque transactions, and a concentrated pool of buyers. Unlike regulated securities, art sales are often private, negotiated, and shrouded in discretion. For the serious investor, this opacity is both a risk and an opportunity—requiring deep relationships, domain expertise, and caution.

Importantly, taste itself is not static. Trends shift, movements fall in and out of favour, and what was once considered avant-garde can become passé. Abstract Expressionism, once the dominant post-war idiom, gave way to Pop Art, then to Conceptualism, then to figurative revivals. The current market sees growing interest in artists from the Global South, in underrepresented narratives, in politically engaged work. These aren't merely aesthetic turns—they reflect broader cultural, social, and geopolitical currents. To understand where art is going, one must read not just art history, but the cultural mood. *Taste is a moving index of collective attention.*

Yet, perhaps the most misunderstood variable in art appreciation is *time.* Unlike tech stocks or commodities, art often requires decades to mature in value. Collectors with vision buy into a career, a thesis, a belief about future relevance. They are rewarded not for speed but for conviction. Short-term flipping—acquiring young artists' works and quickly reselling them—may yield quick gains during frothy periods, but also risks saturating the market and damaging the artist's long-term trajectory. The true investor plays the long game, recognising that art is less about timing the market and more about *understanding how markets remember.*

That memory is curated. Museums, archives, retrospectives—all play a role in cementing legacy. An artist shown at the Venice Biennale or Documenta becomes part of the canon. Their work is written into textbooks, studied in universities, referenced by future generations. That cultural anchoring translates into market durability. It is no coincidence that works from artists included in major museum collections appreciate more consistently than those outside those circles. *Institutions are arbiters of legacy—and legacy drives value.*

So why does art appreciate? Because it is scarce, authenticated, culturally validated, and increasingly seen as a strategic store of wealth. Why does it sometimes not? Because markets lose faith, narratives falter, authenticity fails, or relevance fades. Beauty, while a factor, is secondary to belief—belief in the artist, in their contribution, and in their continued importance. Investing in art, then, is not merely about acquiring objects. It is about participating in a conversation—curated, contested, evolving—and doing so with both intellectual rigour and market intelligence. *The investor who understands this invests not just in art, but in the infrastructure of meaning that surrounds it.*

Taste as Tactic: Cultural Literacy and Asset Selection

In the world of alternative assets—where returns are often interwoven with emotion, story, and status—*taste* is not a luxury. It's a lever of power. Whether curating a wine cellar, selecting contemporary art, or investing in intellectual property, the edge belongs not only to those with capital, but to those who know *what matters, when it matters, and to whom it matters.* In these markets, financial literacy without cultural fluency is like reading music without ever having heard it played.

Cultural literacy is the capacity to detect, decode, and contextualise value in objects whose worth is not strictly financial. A Picasso and a Banksy may both sell for millions, but they operate in different symbolic registers. One is institutionalised historical capital; the other, cultural rebellion commodified. To invest wisely, one must understand not only the supply and demand curves—but also the critical dialogues, curatorial movements, and cultural tides that push certain assets to prominence. It is here that *taste*, properly developed, becomes more than preference. It becomes strategy.

Developing cultural fluency is less about memorising auction results or attending art fairs and more about *learning how networks of meaning are built and transmitted.* An artwork's value is not created in isolation. It's socially constructed—through galleries, critics, collectors, museums, influencers, and the media. Likewise, a Burgundy vintage or a first-edition novel doesn't appreciate simply because it's old. It appreciates because communities have been cultivated around it, because narratives have been reinforced, and because scarcity has been maintained or mythologised. A culturally literate investor asks: *Who is shaping this narrative? How durable is the story? And who believes it enough to pay for it?*

One must also recognise the asymmetry between personal taste and market taste. Many novice investors make the mistake of confusing what they like with what the market will value. The gap between connoisseurship and liquidity can be vast. A photographer's work may be technically brilliant, but if it hasn't entered the institutional ecosystem—shown in major museums, collected by influential patrons, or reviewed by notable critics—it may never command investment-level prices. The same logic applies in literature: a beautifully written novel might go unnoticed in the market if it lacks either cultural visibility or strategic rights management. *Taste, in this context, must be tempered with discipline and pattern recognition.*

Consider the case of Jean-Michel Basquiat. In the 1980s, his work was dismissed by many as graffiti-inspired spectacle. Today, it is among the most coveted by global collectors, often commanding prices exceeding $100 million. What changed? Not just the art, but the *ecosystem around the art*: the curators who championed him, the scholars who canonised him, the collectors who competed for him. Savvy investors recognised early that Basquiat represented not just a talented individual, but a bridge between street culture and institutional validation—a cultural inflection point. Identifying such moments requires more than luck; it demands *cultural pattern recognition.*

The same principles apply in wine. Take Domaine de la Romanée-Conti (DRC), widely considered the pinnacle of Burgundy. Its prices are astronomical not solely because of terroir or craftsmanship, but because it sits at the nexus of rarity, prestige, and legacy. To anticipate the next DRC, investors must watch for emerging vineyards gaining traction with influential sommeliers, collectors, and critics—not just those making technically excellent wine, but those whose *story aligns with shifting global tastes*. The rise of premium Californian or South African wines, for instance, reflects both climatic innovation and cultural repositioning.

In both wine and art, *taste is not static—it's geopolitical.* Cultural capital flows across borders. The rise of Asia's ultra-wealthy has changed the centre of gravity for art sales. Chinese contemporary artists now dominate auction house catalogues, while global wine demand increasingly reflects the palates of emerging markets. Cultural literacy must therefore be *multinational and multilingual*, not provincial or trend-chasing. A collector who understands how Korean pop culture has altered the fashion and music industries will be better positioned to anticipate which visual artists or authors might become globally significant in the next decade.

Yet cultural literacy also means knowing when not to invest. There are periods of exuberance where hype outpaces substance—where asset prices are inflated by social media virality rather than any long-term cultural commitment. The ability to differentiate a flash-in-the-pan trend from a genuine cultural pivot is where taste becomes a shield as well as a sword. For every Banksy who ascends, there are dozens of derivatives that quietly fade. For every natural wine movement that matures, there are others that collapse under the weight of faddishness. *Knowing when to abstain is often as valuable as knowing when to act.*

The mechanisms of validation are also worth decoding. Museums, biennials, literary prizes, and influential critics form the scaffolding of value creation. These institutions don't simply reflect taste—they manufacture it. Understanding who sits on their boards, which artists or vintners they promote, and how they signal value to broader audiences is not a cynical exercise in manipulation. It is a realistic approach to how markets work when taste and economics intersect. The investor who maps these influence networks—who reads catalogues as carefully as earnings reports—will often be several steps ahead of those who rely purely on intuition.

At its highest level, cultural literacy is about *interpretive skill.* It is the ability to read cultural signals, situate them within broader social movements, and project how they might evolve. The investor who saw the political resonance of black art in America before 2020 or who tracked the rise of female vintners in a male-dominated Burgundy system was not only culturally attuned, but financially advantaged. In these markets, *context is alpha.*

Finally, cultural taste must be cultivated intentionally. It is not innate; it is developed. This means studying—not just the markets, but the canons. Read widely. Visit museums. Speak to gallerists. Taste beyond your preferences. Watch how others watch. Cultural literacy grows through immersion, not osmosis. The more you expose yourself to the serious discourse around cultural production, the more fluent—and prescient—you become.

In the end, investing in taste-based assets is not just a financial act, but an epistemological one. It asks: *How do we know what's valuable?* Who decides, and why? The investor who can navigate those questions with clarity, scepticism, and sophistication is better positioned to not only protect their capital, but to participate in shaping the value systems of the future. Taste is not a luxury. It is an asset class of its own—intangible, complex, but deeply powerful when harnessed with precision.

Storage, Curation, and Market Mechanics

The moment an investor acquires a bottle of Romanée-Conti or a canvas attributed to Cy Twombly, they face a less glamorous—but no less essential—challenge: what now? Unlike stocks or bonds, alternative assets like wine and art require not just selection but stewardship. They are tangible, delicate, and context-dependent. Their value is not only a function of intrinsic quality or cultural esteem but also of physical integrity, legal clarity, and transactional fluency. *To own such assets without understanding their operational architecture is to mistake possession for control.*

Storage is the first and most underestimated pillar of asset preservation. For fine wine, it is not merely about temperature—it is about provenance. The most valuable wines are those with an unbroken chain of custody, stored under ideal conditions from château to collector. Storage at 13°C, with 70% humidity, minimal vibration, and complete darkness is not a luxury; it is a requirement. Professional wine storage facilities, such as those offered by Octavian Vaults in the UK or Domaine in the United States, provide tamper-proof environments with full traceability. The investor who stores their bottles at home—however carefully—is injecting uncertainty into the chain of credibility that underpins valuation.

With art, the same principle applies. Climate-controlled storage, often in specialised freeports or bonded warehouses, is essential not just for preservation but also for discretion and tax efficiency. Institutions like the Geneva Freeport offer security, anonymity, and a deferred-tax environment for high-value works. But here too, nuance matters. Art stored indefinitely off-view may retain its physical condition, but it risks cultural invisibility. If a piece is never exhibited, written about, or seen by curators and collectors, its significance may stagnate or erode. *Curation and storage must work in tandem—not as opposites, but as components of strategic visibility.*

Insurance follows logically. Yet many investors underinsure or misunderstand the complexity of valuation in illiquid markets. A painting's market value is not necessarily its insured value. Appraisals should be updated regularly, and policies must be tailored for the asset's medium, condition, and storage location. For wine, breakage, spoilage, and transport risks must be explicitly covered. For art, the risk matrix expands to include theft, fire, and restoration complications. Sophisticated investors work with niche insurers like AXA Art or Hiscox, who understand the specific exposures of cultural assets. *Generic home or contents policies are not only insufficient—they may void coverage entirely.*

Legal structure is another often-overlooked factor. High-value wine or art should rarely be held in an individual's name. Whether through trusts, LLCs, or SPVs (special purpose vehicles), ownership structures must balance asset protection, tax optimisation, and estate planning. In the case of fractional ownership—now increasingly common through platforms like Masterworks (for art) or Cult Wines (for wine portfolios)—clarity over voting rights, liquidity windows, and custodial responsibilities becomes critical. Legal ambiguity is the enemy of long-term value realisation. *Sophistication in legal structuring is not bureaucratic overhead—it is a form of value insulation.*

Resale, meanwhile, is where strategy culminates. The liquidity of a wine or art investment is not guaranteed by the object's quality but by the strength of the resale channel. For wine, global auction houses such as Sotheby's, Christie's, and Zachys offer reach and credibility, but take significant commissions. Secondary platforms like WineBid or LiveTrade provide lower friction, but often lower prices. For private resale, relationships matter—brokers with trusted networks can drive better outcomes than anonymous platforms. With art, galleries and private dealers may offer discretion and strategic placement, but public auction remains the price-setting mechanism of record. Understanding *when and where* to sell—during a retrospective, after an artist's death, amid a cultural revival—is as critical as knowing *what* to sell. *Timing is not just a market call—it is a curatorial decision.*

Yet curation, properly understood, extends beyond resale positioning. It is the ongoing management of an asset's contextual value. A wine collection with depth across vintages and producers has more narrative coherence—and more resale gravity—than a scattershot assortment of trophy bottles. An art collection that reflects a theme, movement, or scholarly relevance attracts curators, lenders, and institutional buyers in ways that singular pieces cannot. Curation is what transforms a storage unit into a collection. It is how collectors build influence, not just portfolios. *Tasteful accumulation becomes capital when shaped by vision.*

Even digital infrastructure plays a role. Provenance and condition must be documented in ways that survive ownership transfer. For art, this means certificates of authenticity, condition reports, and high-resolution imaging. For wine, it includes purchase receipts, storage statements, and sometimes even bottling line traceability. Increasingly, blockchain is entering the space, offering tamper-proof title records. But while technology enhances transparency, it cannot replace discipline. *Documentation is not optional. It is the language in which value is negotiated.*

Critically, one must also account for the costs of ownership. Storage fees, insurance premiums, advisory costs, and transactional commissions can erode returns if not integrated into portfolio analysis. Unlike passive index funds, these assets require ongoing capital allocation. Moreover, they demand time, attention, and knowledge. Investors drawn to the romance of a Château Lafite or a Richter canvas must also embrace the operational rigour those assets command. *Ownership here is a vocation, not a hobby.*

Finally, ethics and regulation are entering the picture with new intensity. Cultural patrimony laws restrict the export of artworks from certain countries. Wine fraud and counterfeiting have led to prosecutions and tighter scrutiny. The investor must be aware not just of financial and legal mechanics, but of cultural and regulatory boundaries. *Due diligence is not merely financial—it is moral and geopolitical.*

To invest in wine or art is to hold something that embodies both value and vulnerability. These are not idle assets. They are dynamic, physical, and context-rich. They can appreciate dramatically—but only under the right conditions, with the right protections, and through the right channels. Storage, curation, and market mechanics are not ancillary details. They are the infrastructure of belief that allows the intangible—taste, rarity, beauty—to be converted into capital. To master these dimensions is not to remove risk, but to understand where it resides, how it moves, and how it might one day be turned—intelligently—into return.

Chapter 7
The New Acre—Farmland, Forests, and Eco-Conscious Wealth

Land has always been the quiet foundation beneath civilisation's most enduring fortunes. Long before derivatives, tech stocks, or compound-interest accounts, there was soil, water, trees, and seasons. For millennia, wealth was measured in acres, and power in the ability to control what grew upon them. Today, amidst digital assets and financial abstractions, capital is quietly circling back to these primal foundations. Farmland and forests—once dismissed as slow, provincial, or sentimental—are now being recognised as finely tuned instruments for resilient, regenerative, and ethically aligned wealth creation.

This chapter examines why the oldest asset class may paradoxically represent the newest frontier for capital. Nostalgia plays little part in this shift; data drives it. Institutional investors, family offices, and sovereign funds are committing billions to arable land, timber tracts, and conservation-linked real assets—not out of romance, but because the long-term fundamentals are compelling. Population growth, climate uncertainty, and fragile supply chains have elevated the strategic importance of productive ecosystems. Meanwhile, regulatory, technological, and philosophical frameworks governing land ownership are evolving, unlocking both alpha and purpose.

Understanding the investment case for farmland demands thinking across time horizons that conventional portfolios often ignore. Cropland generates more than food; it produces income, diversifies risk, and can act as a hedge. Whether leased to operators, cultivated for cash crops, or held for appreciation in rapidly urbanising corridors, farmland offers stability rarely seen in public equities. Headlines may trumpet wheat futures or seasonal droughts, yet the underlying trend is clear: supply is finite, demand global and rising. As institutional capital expands in this space, smaller investors must adopt strategy and discernment to access meaningful opportunity.

Yet to regard farmland solely in economic terms is to overlook its complexity. Fields are ecosystems—biomes alive with interdependent processes. Investors increasingly price land not merely by yield per acre, but by regenerative practices, carbon sequestration potential, and biodiversity metrics. Sustainability has shifted from marketing rhetoric to balance-sheet logic. Premium tenants, grants, and higher resale valuations now reward attention to soil health and environmental stewardship. The "green" in greenfield has never carried more strategic significance.

Timberland occupies a similarly underappreciated space. Trees grow biologically, compounding in mass rather than simply appreciating with inflation. This creates a form of intrinsic value that operates independently of market cycles. Properly managed, timber can be harvested sustainably in perpetuity, offering both recurring income and deferred capital gains. Unlike many other assets, timber maintains utility: it feeds housing, packaging, energy, and infrastructure—sectors impervious to digital disruption.

The true sophistication of land investing lies in curation—how parcels are acquired, managed, and transitioned. Returns are not dictated solely by weather or soil fertility; legal frameworks, tenant dynamics, water rights, infrastructure access, zoning policies, and environmental regulations all play decisive roles. High-functioning investors approach land not as a passive store of value, but as a responsive platform. Decisions about crops, leases, organic adoption, or climate-risk mitigation can shift outcomes dramatically.

Land also engages investors psychologically in ways few other assets can. It is tangible, walkable, real. Unlike securities or digital tokens, one can stand upon it, build upon it, cultivate it. This tangibility fosters conviction, yet can also invite sentimentality and illiquidity. Savvy investors balance emotional attachment with analytical rigor, embracing both stewardship and strategy.

A particularly urgent dimension of modern land investment is the integration of environmental objectives with capital goals. Climate-aligned vehicles—reforestation bonds, agroecology funds, and conservation easements—now blend measurable ecological benefit with financial return. These are no longer niche impact plays. Large institutions, from BlackRock to TIAA to Norway's sovereign wealth fund, invest in sustainable land strategies not out of altruism, but rational calculation. The alignment of ecological resilience with economic durability has crystallised into a strategic thesis, supported by climate models, yield projections, and risk assessments.

This chapter unpacks these dynamics in layered detail. It begins with the foundational case for land in a modern portfolio—not merely as a hedge, but as a core asset capable of producing cash flow, appreciation, and strategic optionality. It examines how farmland generates value through rental models, crop cycles, commodity pricing, and water access. From there, it turns to timber, explaining how tree growth and harvest cycles offer one of the most elegant inflation hedges available to long-horizon investors. Throughout, sustainability is emphasised not simply as ethics, but as competitive advantage increasingly embedded in valuation models.

By chapter's end, readers will understand not just how land performs, but why it endures. They will gain the vocabulary, mental models, and strategic insight to evaluate opportunities with discernment. In a world dominated by digitisation and volatility, land offers quiet power—assets that grow silently, root deeply, and reward the patient. Land is not old-fashioned. It is enduring. And for those with the right perspective, it is far more than dirt—it is leverage.

The Oldest Asset: Why Land Still Matters –

Land is not just a location; it is a ledger of civilisation's ambitions, failures, and reinventions. Empires have risen and collapsed over access to fertile soil. Nations have drawn their borders, waged wars, and defined laws with land as both battlefield and prize. Long before the concept of "asset class" existed, ownership of land signified permanence, status, and strategic advantage. Today, amid the churn of global volatility, farmland is re-emerging not merely as a nostalgic nod to wealth-building tradition, but as a structurally sound, inflation-resistant, and increasingly coveted investment vehicle—quietly outpacing more celebrated sectors of modern finance.

What makes land uniquely durable is its blend of physical utility and limited supply. Every other investable asset—stocks, bonds, even gold—can be created, split, or reissued. Land, by contrast, cannot be manufactured or duplicated. There is only so much arable land on Earth, and its productive capacity is under mounting pressure from climate change, urban sprawl, soil degradation, and competing land uses. As demand for food, fibre, and fuel escalates with population growth, farmland has acquired a new strategic profile—not just for farmers, but for pension funds, sovereign investors, and environmentally conscious allocators seeking yield with a lower correlation to traditional markets.

The appeal is structural, not speculative. Farmland generates returns through three primary mechanisms: rental income from tenant farmers, operating profits from crop sales (where the landowner farms directly or via joint ventures), and long-term appreciation in land value. Unlike equities, whose value can be severed from fundamentals by sentiment or hype, land's productivity offers a baseline of tangible economic output. Corn, wheat, soy, or avocados are not theories—they are tradeable commodities with futures markets, supply chains, and end-user demand. Even in a recession, people eat. In this sense, farmland behaves more like an infrastructure asset: essential, enduring, and linked to non-discretionary consumption.

What makes the farmland investment case more compelling now is its resilience during periods of inflation. As input costs rise and currency value erodes, food prices typically climb—creating a natural hedge for agricultural assets. The historical data supports this: during the stagflation era of the 1970s, American farmland posted some of its strongest real returns. That pattern has not gone unnoticed by institutions. Over the past decade, major players like TIAA, the Harvard Endowment, and Canada's PSP Investments have significantly expanded their agricultural holdings, citing diversification benefits, inflation protection, and ESG alignment as core drivers. Their scale and patience make them formidable competitors, but they also professionalise the sector, bringing rigour and transparency to what was once a local, relationship-driven market.

At the same time, this influx of capital has catalysed innovation in farmland investing vehicles. Gone are the days when the only way to own farmland was to buy a tract, learn agriculture, and hope for a good harvest. Today, investors can access the asset class through private equity funds, farmland REITs, tokenised land platforms, and co-ownership syndicates that manage properties on behalf of passive stakeholders. These structures offer fractional exposure, geographic diversification, and professional oversight, reducing the operational complexity and capital intensity that have historically deterred smaller investors. The result is a democratisation of access—but also a sharpening of the knowledge requirements needed to compete intelligently.

Understanding farmland as an investment, however, requires more than enthusiasm for hard assets or a romantic attachment to the countryside. It demands technical fluency across multiple domains: soil science, water rights, crop rotation strategies, input cost dynamics, trade policy, local taxation, and climate risk. No two parcels are the same, even within the same county. A hectare of black loam in Iowa carries a different risk-return profile than a vineyard in Mendoza, an almond orchard in California, or a rice paddy in Vietnam. Evaluating farmland requires not only geographic insight but also operational literacy—understanding how yield per acre, drainage, infrastructure access, and pest resilience affect both cash flow and appreciation.

Moreover, the legal and political environment is crucial. Land rights are among the most contested and complex areas of law. In emerging markets, land titling may be incomplete or subject to political reversal. In developed markets, zoning restrictions, conservation easements, and tax treatments all influence profitability. Institutional investors often employ full-time legal teams and agronomists to navigate these layers. Private investors must either develop comparable fluency or partner with managers who already possess it. This is not an arena for casual speculation. Farmland rewards rigour, patience, and local expertise over short-termism or broad-stroke optimism.

Another layer of complexity—and opportunity—is the accelerating interplay between farmland and climate policy. As governments expand incentives for carbon sequestration, soil regeneration, and sustainable practices, farmland is being recast as a platform for environmental services, not just food production. Programmes that pay landowners for planting cover crops, reducing fertiliser runoff, or adopting no-till methods are creating new revenue streams while enhancing land health. Emerging carbon credit markets are further monetising soil-based carbon capture, with companies like Indigo Ag and Nori facilitating transactions between farmers and corporates seeking to offset emissions. The investor who understands these trends is not just buying land—they're buying a call option on the future of sustainability-linked finance.

Crucially, this transformation is shifting how land is valued. It's no longer just about yield and price per acre. Increasingly, buyers are looking at regenerative potential, biodiversity scores, water resilience, and proximity to climate-stable zones. Land with resilient ecological characteristics is commanding a premium—and is more likely to retain value in a world of accelerating environmental volatility. This is where ethical investing and financial prudence converge. Owning land that heals ecosystems is not only morally defensible; it is rapidly becoming the smarter economic bet.

For all its attractions, farmland is not a utopia. It carries real risks. Drought, pests, commodity price crashes, trade wars, labour shortages—these are operational headwinds that cannot be diversified away. Moreover, land is illiquid. Selling a farm is not like offloading shares on a Monday morning. Transactions can take months, require local knowledge, and be deeply affected by timing, sentiment, or regulatory delays. Investors must weigh the trade-off between stability and liquidity, and structure their portfolios accordingly.

But the most underappreciated risk is managerial: poor stewardship. Land that is over-farmed, under-maintained, or misaligned with market demand can degrade rapidly in both ecological and financial terms. Passive ownership without oversight can lead to capital erosion masked by surface-level appreciation. To treat farmland as a commodity is to misunderstand its nature. It is a living, breathing asset. Its value is not fixed—it is shaped, cultivated, and either enhanced or exhausted by every decision made upon it.

What, then, should the thoughtful investor take from all this? That farmland is not just a place to park capital—it is a place to grow it, patiently and strategically. That land is not merely real estate, but a productive system embedded in climate, community, and global supply chains. That owning a piece of the Earth's productive surface is both a privilege and a responsibility—one that, handled well, offers extraordinary resilience, returns, and relevance in a world hungry for both stability and sustainability.

Farmland is not a hedge against the modern economy; it is a foundation beneath it. And as more investors come to realise that the future of food, water, and carbon are also the future of finance, the soil beneath our feet may again become the bedrock of wealth creation. Not because it is trendy, but because it is timeless.

From Soil to Yield: How Farmland Generates Returns-

There is a quiet elegance in the way farmland generates wealth—not through speculative hype or financial engineering, but through the compounding rhythm of seasons, yields, and long-term stewardship. Unlike asset classes that trade on narrative or volatility, farmland earns its keep through a fundamentally productive cycle. Crops grow. Rents are collected. Land appreciates. And through this interplay of biology, contract, and capital, the soil becomes an engine of financial continuity in a world often defined by noise.

To understand how farmland generates returns, one must look beneath the surface—literally and structurally. At its core, farmland produces value through three interconnected streams: *rental income*, *operating yield*, and *capital appreciation*. Each offers its own risk-reward profile, influenced by geographic conditions, commodity cycles, tenant quality, and macroeconomic forces. But all three are grounded in the land's intrinsic capacity to produce something tangible, edible, and necessary. This is investment at its most elemental.

Rental income forms the backbone of many farmland portfolios, particularly for passive investors who lease their land to local farmers under fixed or variable agreements. Fixed-rent models offer predictable cash flow, with tenants paying a set amount per acre regardless of harvest outcomes. Variable leases, by contrast, link payments to commodity prices or yield levels, giving the landowner upside exposure to strong seasons—but also exposure to downside risk. Hybrid arrangements, including base-plus-percentage leases, attempt to strike a balance. Institutional investors typically prefer structured leases with reliable tenants and long-term agreements, seeing them as a proxy for fixed income in a diversified portfolio.

Yet while rental contracts provide stability, the true financial engine of farmland lies in its operating returns—especially when investors are directly involved in production. Here, the landowner either farms the land themselves, engages an operator, or participates in joint ventures that allow for more control over inputs, crop selection, and cost management. Operating farms can generate significantly higher returns than leased parcels, but they also introduce layers of operational complexity, weather exposure, and commodity risk. A well-run corn or soybean operation in the American Midwest, for instance, might deliver annual net returns of 4% to 7% after expenses, depending on scale and market conditions.

Capital appreciation, the third pillar of farmland return, operates on longer horizons. It is influenced by both intrinsic and extrinsic factors—soil health, water access, zoning potential, and broader demographic or economic trends. Areas on the urban fringe often experience rising land values due to development pressures, while high-quality agricultural regions benefit from scarcity, productivity, and increasing global food demand. Unlike equities or REITs, farmland doesn't reprice daily. Its value accrues slowly, with step changes driven by market cycles, inflation, and shifts in global agricultural policy. Over time, however, appreciation often outpaces headline inflation, offering a durable hedge against currency debasement.

Importantly, these return streams are not uniform across markets. Farmland in New Zealand behaves differently than wheat fields in Saskatchewan or vineyards in Bordeaux. Climate, regulation, infrastructure, and commodity exposure all shape the performance profile. Investors must engage not only with macro trends—such as rising protein consumption in Asia or climate volatility—but also with local agronomic realities. The best farmland investment is not simply the most picturesque, but the most productive relative to its cost base, resilience, and market access.

A growing number of agricultural funds and platforms are attempting to democratise access to this asset class. From crowdfunding models that pool capital for small parcels, to billion-dollar institutional funds acquiring thousands of acres at a time, farmland is no longer the domain of local families and agricultural dynasties alone. This shift has introduced liquidity, data, and professional management to the space—but it has also invited speculation, greenwashing, and capital misallocation. Investors must tread carefully, distinguishing between marketing narratives and measurable value.

For instance, regenerative agriculture is often promoted as a panacea—a way to enhance soil health, sequester carbon, and produce returns with a moral halo. While some regenerative practices do improve long-term soil productivity and ecosystem resilience, they are not universally profitable nor equally applicable. Without deep agronomic insight, investors risk misreading the impact of cover crops, rotational grazing, or low-till methods. Similarly, carbon credits attached to farmland are still governed by immature markets, fragmented standards, and uncertain policy support. These may provide upside in the future, but they should not be treated as baseline assumptions in cash flow models.

From a financial structuring perspective, farmland sits at the intersection of real estate and private equity. It is an illiquid asset, with limited secondary markets and long holding periods—yet it can produce stable yield and capital growth if professionally managed. Sophisticated investors typically use limited partnerships or agricultural REITs to gain exposure, balancing direct ownership with operational outsourcing. Some choose to hedge commodity exposure using futures markets, while others diversify by crop type, geography, or water access to smooth volatility.

Critically, farmland returns are increasingly correlated with global themes: climate stress, water scarcity, food security, and shifting diets. As plant-based protein gains traction, certain crops—like pulses and oilseeds—may rise in value. Climate change, meanwhile, is redrawing agricultural maps, making water rights, elevation, and weather patterns integral to underwriting decisions. Areas once considered marginal may become arable; others may face yield collapse. Investors who succeed in farmland will be those who combine asset-level due diligence with systems-level foresight.

Perhaps the most underestimated driver of farmland performance is stewardship. Soil is not static. It responds to how it is treated, farmed, and protected. Investors focused only on yield risk undermining long-term fertility and value. Those who integrate soil testing, nutrient management, and sustainability metrics into their strategies tend to outperform over time. As agricultural technology continues to evolve—from precision irrigation to biological pest control—the future of farmland investment will hinge not just on acquisition, but on optimisation.

Ultimately, farmland's appeal lies in its contradiction: it is both ancient and increasingly relevant. It is slow capital in a fast-money world. And yet, precisely because of that, it offers something rare—returns grounded in reality, productivity linked to biology, and wealth grown from the ground up. For investors seeking resilience, utility, and meaning, few assets carry the same mix of legacy and leverage. The soil, it turns out, still pays.

Trees, Timber, and Time Horizons

At a glance, a stand of trees may not look like capital. Yet to those who understand its economics, a managed forest represents one of the most elegant, patient, and biologically aligned investment models available. Timberland doesn't just preserve wealth—it *grows* it. Literally. With each passing season, trees mature, increase in volume, and compound in value, delivering a unique intersection of natural growth and financial yield. For the investor attuned to long durations, ecological cycles, and inflation protection, timberland offers a compelling blend of resilience and regeneration.

The structure of a timberland investment differs fundamentally from traditional financial assets. A bond pays fixed interest; an equity offers dividends and volatility; but a forest quietly appreciates, not through market speculation, but through biological expansion. The trunk thickens. The tree adds rings. Cubic metres increase. And the longer one waits—up to a species-specific biological ceiling—the more the timber is worth. *Compounding, in this context, is not metaphorical—it is organic.*

This growth curve is what underpins timberland's financial architecture. The value of a tree rises not linearly but exponentially, as both its usable volume and commercial grade improve with age. For instance, a pine planted today may be worth very little after five years, moderately valuable at fifteen, and highly prized at thirty or forty—particularly if it meets the specifications for sawtimber rather than pulpwood. Each delay in harvest means a bigger, better product—albeit with the costs of time, management, and risk exposure along the way. This embedded optionality is what gives timberland its asymmetric return potential: the longer the hold, the greater the growth, assuming ecological and market conditions cooperate.

Returns from timberland generally stem from three sources: *biological growth*, *price appreciation*, and *land value escalation*. Biological growth refers to the increase in wood volume and merchantability. Price appreciation follows cycles in global demand—particularly from housing, construction, and paper industries. And land value can rise independently, especially near urbanising areas or with alternative use potential. Combined, these drivers have produced historically robust, low-volatility returns. Data from the National Council of Real Estate Investment Fiduciaries (NCREIF) shows that US timberland has delivered long-term average annual returns of approximately 8%—often with low correlation to equities and bonds.

Crucially, timberland also offers a natural hedge against inflation. Wood prices tend to rise with general price levels, particularly because timber is a key input into housing and infrastructure—both sectors that experience cost inflation during boom cycles. At the same time, trees continue to grow regardless of market fluctuations. Their intrinsic value accumulation provides an underlying buffer against devaluation. This makes timberland especially attractive in periods of macroeconomic instability, currency erosion, or stagflation, where traditional assets falter but tangible, productive land retains its allure.

However, timberland is not a passive asset. Managing a forest requires expertise, infrastructure, and long-term planning. Variables such as thinning schedules, pest control, fire risk, and replanting regimes all shape the asset's future productivity. Moreover, timing the harvest is both a science and an art. Sell too early, and the investor forgoes compounding. Wait too long, and the stand may become over-mature or vulnerable. Sophisticated investors integrate silvicultural models with market forecasts to determine optimal rotation cycles, blending biological data with economic indicators.

Geography also plays a significant role. Timber markets are hyper-local, influenced by mill proximity, transportation costs, regional species, and export infrastructure. For example, Southern pine in the United States offers a different return profile than eucalyptus plantations in Brazil or Douglas fir forests in British Columbia. Each region has its own climatic risks—droughts, hurricanes, beetle infestations—and regulatory environments. Consequently, diversification across geographies and species is as critical in timber as in any financial portfolio.

Investors typically access timberland through three main routes: direct ownership, timber investment management organisations (TIMOs), or public timberland REITs. Direct ownership allows for full control and potentially higher margins but demands operational capacity and scale. TIMOs pool capital from institutions or high-net-worth individuals, offering professional management and strategic diversification. Public REITs, like Weyerhaeuser or Rayonier, offer liquidity and dividends but are also subject to public market sentiment, which can obscure the fundamental performance of the underlying land.

A more recent evolution in the sector is the integration of timberland with *environmental, social, and governance (ESG)* objectives. Trees are carbon sinks; forests provide biodiversity and water protection; sustainable harvesting creates rural employment. As climate pressures rise and capital seeks alignment with low-carbon assets, timberland is being re-evaluated not just as a resource play but as a *climate-resilient infrastructure asset.* Some investors are now layering carbon offset strategies into their timber portfolios—either by extending harvest timelines (and thus increasing sequestration) or enrolling in formal carbon markets. While still a developing area, these overlays may enhance both financial return and reputational value.

There are, of course, limitations. Timberland is illiquid by nature. Sale cycles are long, buyers are niche, and valuation is inherently appraised rather than marked to market. Catastrophic events—wildfires, blights, geopolitical disruptions—can wipe out years of growth. Insurance helps, but only partially. Moreover, timber markets are cyclical. Periods of overplanting, housing downturns, or trade barriers can suppress prices for years. Patience is not optional; it is integral to the model.

From a psychological perspective, timberland demands a rare kind of investor temperament: one comfortable with slow progress, delayed gratification, and compounding outcomes that are measured in decades rather than quarters. In a world addicted to immediacy, that mindset is contrarian—and valuable. Timber doesn't tweet, spike, or crash. It grows quietly, predictably, often imperceptibly—until, one day, the stand is harvest-ready and the value is realised in full.

This long duration is not a weakness. It is the essence of the asset's strength. While algorithmic traders chase milliseconds, and venture funds gamble on exponential failure rates, timberland builds wealth the old-fashioned way: through biology, discipline, and the slow alchemy of photosynthesis. In doing so, it offers not just return, but perspective. A forest reminds the investor of time's true shape. It teaches stewardship. It rewards care. And it remains, amid volatility and noise, one of the few assets that doesn't merely represent value—it *grows* it.

Sustainability as Strategy

Sustainability is no longer an altruistic gesture made at the expense of return; it is now a material driver of long-term performance. In land ownership and stewardship, the alignment between ecological sensitivity and financial resilience is becoming not only visible, but quantifiable. The idea that caring for the land compromises yield is increasingly defunct. Instead, ESG-oriented frameworks—once seen as niche or compliance-driven—are now being embedded into the core thesis of asset managers, institutional funds, and individual investors alike. *Sustainability has moved from the periphery to the portfolio.*

Land, particularly farmland and forest, offers one of the most direct ways to apply sustainability as an investment lever. Unlike financial instruments, which abstract impact across layers of intermediaries, land connects investor intent with real outcomes—on soil, water, biodiversity, and carbon. If managed regeneratively, it can sequester carbon, rebuild topsoil, improve watershed function, and foster local economies. If degraded, it becomes a liability. The choices an owner makes are not just moral but materially consequential. The land either appreciates with ecological vitality or erodes alongside environmental neglect.

What sets sustainable land investment apart is that its benefits accrue in layered forms. On the one hand, you have the tangible: improved yields from healthy soil, higher timber volume from biodiverse forests, reduced input costs through organic methods, and better resistance to climate shocks. On the other, there are intangible but powerful premiums: increased buyer interest, eligibility for ESG-aligned capital, lower regulatory risk, and reputational value in a market increasingly attuned to ethical provenance. These are no longer soft metrics; they are real, investable signals that shape asset pricing and market access.

The growth of ESG mandates across institutional capital pools has also reconfigured the demand side. Pension funds, sovereign wealth funds, and endowments now operate under explicit sustainability targets. For landowners and operators, this means that integrating ESG practices isn't a branding exercise—it's an access strategy. If your asset isn't compliant with ESG reporting frameworks such as

GRESB, SASB, or TCFD, it may be screened out before it's even considered. Moreover, ESG integration affects exit value: land with traceable sustainability credentials can command a premium at sale, while that which lacks them may be discounted or penalised.

Carbon markets have further intensified the link between sustainability and strategy. Timberland and farmland with verifiable carbon sequestration capacity are now eligible for carbon credits, which can be sold in compliance or voluntary markets. These credits represent a new revenue stream layered on top of traditional operations. A forest that is selectively harvested or a pasture that is rotated regeneratively can, with proper monitoring, earn income not only from product output but from ecological service. This shift reframes land not just as a commodity source but as a climate asset—an infrastructure of planetary function.

Yet monetising sustainability is not automatic. It requires evidence, verification, and rigorous practice. Investors must move beyond performative ESG checklists to genuine operational integration. For example, simply reducing fertiliser use on a farm is not sufficient. Has the soil organic matter improved over time? Is biodiversity increasing? Are water tables stable? The value of sustainability is unlocked not through intention, but through measurable, longitudinal outcomes. This demands robust data infrastructure, local knowledge, and often a blend of agronomic science and ecological literacy. Without it, ESG becomes theatre.

A further dimension to sustainability strategy is policy alignment. Governments across the globe are shifting from subsidy models to incentive structures based on environmental performance. In the UK, the Environmental Land Management Scheme (ELMS) links farm support payments to ecosystem services. In the EU, the Common Agricultural Policy is being recast with green architecture at its centre. In the US, conservation reserve programmes, tax benefits for conservation easements, and state-level climate grants are pushing landowners to integrate public benefit with private ownership. Strategic investors will track and align with these movements—not react to them post hoc.

Equally important is how sustainability influences operational risk. Climate change is no longer an abstract horizon but a set of immediate variables—heat stress, drought volatility, flood risk, pest migration—that materially affect land value. A parcel that may have been productive under past norms may become marginal under new ones. Conversely, a property with adaptive capacity—access to water, diversified species, shade structures, and resilience planning—can outperform. ESG in this sense is not optional—it is risk management by another name. And those who adopt it early will be better positioned to weather both environmental and market shocks.

Culturally, the framing of sustainability is also evolving. Investors are beginning to see that environmental consciousness doesn't mean retreating from profit but redefining it. It is possible—and increasingly necessary—to pursue *regenerative alpha*: returns that stem from restoration, not extraction. A walnut orchard planted on degraded land, managed with cover crops and pollinator corridors, can yield strong income, enhanced carbon sequestration, and better long-term soil viability. That is not charity. That is foresight.

Some tensions remain. The commodification of nature—turning trees, wetlands, or carbon into financial products—raises real questions about fairness, sovereignty, and access. Indigenous land rights, rural equity, and ecological limits must all be part of a serious sustainability conversation. Investors who ignore these dimensions may face backlash, reputational risk, or even stranded assets in future regulatory environments. Ethical due diligence must accompany financial diligence.

Moreover, sustainability as strategy requires a shift in time horizons. Many ecological payoffs occur over longer cycles than traditional quarterly or even annual reporting allows. Patience becomes part of the performance model. Managers must recalibrate both their metrics and their mindset: not what changed last month, but what improved over five years. Not just how much revenue was made, but whether the ecosystem function is more robust than before. This demands a culture of stewardship—not just strategy.

In sum, sustainability is not a sector—it is a lens. And through it, land emerges not just as a passive holding, but as an active agent of financial, ecological, and cultural transformation. For those prepared to engage seriously, with rigour and humility, sustainability becomes a source of competitive advantage—an edge rooted not in arbitrage, but in alignment. The future of land investment will be written not only by spreadsheets, but by those who understand that long-term value is grown, not extracted.

Chapter 8
Digital Rarity—NFTs, Virtual Goods, and Web3 Assets

Ownership has always dictated the rhythms of economics, but the digital era compels us to reconsider its meaning entirely. For centuries, value was anchored in the tangible—gold, land, artwork, bonds, buildings. Scarcity, institutional recognition, and enforceable rights conferred confidence. But what becomes of ownership when value is untethered from matter and encoded in ones and zeros? In the realm of NFTs, tokenised assets, and Web3-native goods, digital rarity has emerged as the new frontier—not because the underlying technology is novel, but because the psychology of possession is evolving.

To dismiss NFTs as mere speculation is to overlook a profound shift. Certainly, prices have been inflated beyond intrinsic worth, and irrational exuberance has run rampant. Yet beneath the volatility lies a signal that demands attention: the codification of digital provenance as a foundation for asset legitimacy. NFTs are not simply images or sound files—they are programmable proofs of authenticity, uniqueness, and ownership, embedded immutably in code. This subtle but transformative change alters not just how we value digital media, but how we conceive property itself.

The architecture of scarcity in the digital sphere is paradoxical. The internet was built on abundance; anything uploaded could be copied ad infinitum. Scarcity, traditionally enforced by law or resource limits, was irrelevant. NFTs invert that paradigm. Scarcity is now algorithmic, transparent, and enforceable via smart contracts and cryptography. Metadata, chain-of-ownership history, and minting protocols confer value in ways that were previously inconceivable.

NFTs are also cultural instruments. They function as social signals, intersecting identity, status, and speculation. A Bored Ape or CryptoPunk is far more than a cartoon; it is a badge of membership, an assertion of taste, and, often, a token of early participation. The psychological dynamics mirror luxury markets: utility is secondary to what the item communicates about its holder. Some NFTs even generate recurring revenue through embedded resale royalties, blending symbolic capital with financial return.

Yet the question of ownership is complex. Legal frameworks remain inconsistent and opaque. Purchasing an NFT rarely confers copyright or reproduction rights unless explicitly stipulated. The token may reside in a decentralised ledger, but the artwork itself might live on a centralised server, vulnerable to disappearance. Investors must distinguish between possessing a digital reference and possessing the underlying work. Courts worldwide have yet to converge on clear standards, leaving legal ambiguity a persistent challenge.

Taxation introduces additional complications. Jurisdictions differ on whether NFTs are classified as collectibles, securities, commodities, or intangible property, each with distinct implications for capital gains, income tax, and VAT. Cross-border transactions and pseudonymous wallets further complicate compliance. Many early entrants to the NFT market now face audits or retroactive tax obligations, not from wrongdoing, but because regulatory frameworks lagged behind market adoption.

Beyond mechanics, NFTs invite philosophical reflection. What does it mean to "own" something visible to all yet controlled by one? In the analogue world, possession and control are intertwined. In the digital sphere, visibility and authority are decoupled. Screenshots can replicate NFTs endlessly, yet only the wallet holding the private key can sell, stake, or validate authenticity. Scarcity here is psychological, social, and anchored in consensus, not concealment.

This opens avenues for cultural innovation. NFTs may become tools for collective memory, creative legacies, or instruments of protest. Ukrainian artists have used them to document wartime narratives; marginalised creators bypass traditional gatekeepers through tokenised distribution. The technology enables permanence without institutional permission, challenging traditional hierarchies of ownership, curation, and recognition.

Scepticism remains essential. The early NFT market was rife with hype-driven projects, influencer-fuelled pumps, and fleeting "utility" promises that rarely materialised. Liquidity evaporated, Discord communities emptied, and floor prices collapsed. These experiences illustrate the fragility of digital value when divorced from thoughtful design, long-term engagement, or substantive utility.

This chapter does not seek to evangelise nor condemn. It examines the anatomy of digital value with a critical lens, exploring how tokens acquire significance—technically, legally, and socially—and whether that value can endure. We unpack smart contract standards like ERC-721 and ERC-1155, consider how metadata and provenance influence liquidity, and analyse case studies of both success and failure. The discussion extends to DAOs and tokenised identity, revealing how digital ownership structures are evolving and reshaping notions of reputation, trust, and belonging.

Above all, the reader is encouraged to transcend simplistic binaries of hype versus scam or boom versus bust. NFTs and virtual goods represent a laboratory for rethinking value, trust, and cultural capital in a digitally native economy. Like any asset class, they require discernment, scepticism, and imagination; like any serious investment, they demand not merely capital, but comprehension and conviction. This chapter equips readers with the tools to navigate both.

Tokens as Trophies: Rethinking Ownership in the Digital Age

Ownership, once a concrete act defined by possession of the physical, is undergoing a redefinition in the context of digital scarcity. Non-fungible tokens (NFTs) represent a radical departure from traditional models of asset holding, not only because they exist entirely in digital form, but because their value is anchored in visibility, identity, and social signalling. NFTs are not merely technological novelties or digital files. They are markers of taste, economic conviction, and subcultural affiliation. They function more like trophies than commodities—badges of participation, risk-taking, and, increasingly, belonging.

The psychology of NFTs begins with a fundamental shift in how value is perceived. Traditional ownership—of a house, a painting, or a book—is about exclusivity of access. Digital assets invert this notion. NFTs are visible to all, ownable by one, and valuable because of their public accessibility. Everyone can see the artwork. Only one wallet address holds the verified token. This inversion—ownership without concealment—represents a new kind of prestige economy: one where status is conferred not through privacy, but through publicly auditable possession.

The earliest successful NFTs capitalised on this logic. CryptoPunks, minted in 2017, were simple 8-bit portraits algorithmically generated and distributed for free. Today, they trade for hundreds of thousands to millions of dollars. Not because of their artistic merit, but because they were *first*. Their status derives from their role in the history of digital ownership. They are not just images; they are proof that the owner understood something early—about culture, technology, or attention. Like rare stamps or first-edition books, their value is historical and symbolic more than utilitarian.

This symbolic capital extends into communities. NFT projects often promise not only aesthetic appeal but access—Discord channels, exclusive events, whitelist privileges, governance rights. Holding a specific NFT becomes a form of identity verification within a subculture. The Bored Ape Yacht Club exemplifies this. It is not merely a collection of cartoon primates; it is a social network, a branding ecosystem, and a signalling layer all at once. Celebrities from Stephen Curry to Eminem have bought in, not for the artwork per se, but to affiliate with the aesthetic and ethos of digital risk and rebellion.

Yet this ecosystem is not without its contradictions. NFTs purport to democratise ownership, yet the market quickly stratified into haves and have-nots. Whales accumulated collections, influencers dictated floor prices, and newcomers were often priced out or left holding illiquid assets. Scarcity was coded, not organic. Projects minted 10,000 unique tokens not because of conceptual necessity but because the model worked. What began as innovation rapidly ossified into formula.

The speculative element exacerbates this divide. NFTs are treated as investment vehicles, often with little regard for their aesthetic or cultural worth. Flip culture—buy low, list high—dominates. The psychological profile of many NFT buyers more closely resembles gamblers than collectors. This introduces volatility not just in pricing, but in community coherence. Projects that fail to sustain hype see rapid drop-offs in engagement. Value evaporates when belief dissipates. And in the absence of fundamentals—cash flow, usage, dividends—belief is everything.

But to reduce NFTs to speculation misses their broader function. They are also creative primitives—building blocks for new forms of storytelling, ownership, and interaction. Musicians, filmmakers, and authors are experimenting with tokenised royalties, fan-funded production, and embedded resale rights. Visual artists can, for the first time, enforce royalties on secondary sales through code, bypassing traditional gallery systems. This reconfigures the economics of creativity, shifting power from intermediaries to makers and communities.

This decentralisation of value creation also creates challenges. Quality control is difficult. The same openness that allows artists to thrive independently also enables scams, plagiarism, and derivative spam. The barrier to entry is low—often just a minting fee and a wallet address. As a result, digital marketplaces are saturated with content of wildly varying integrity. Curation becomes essential, and in a decentralised ecosystem, this role is often filled by social consensus or algorithmic filtering, not institutional gatekeepers. This introduces new biases and blind spots, some technical, others cultural.

The NFT as a "trophy" is also not immune to cultural backlash. For many, NFTs represent digital indulgence in a time of ecological and social crisis. Critics point to energy-intensive blockchains (though this has improved with Ethereum's move to proof-of-stake), celebrity cash grabs, and the erosion of artistic quality in favour of marketability. These critiques are not entirely unfounded. But they also reveal a deeper discomfort: we are reconfiguring the grammar of ownership in real time, and the vocabulary is still unfamiliar.

Where traditional trophies are static—the medal, the certificate, the framed photograph—digital trophies are dynamic. They can evolve, unlock benefits, grant governance rights, or transform through time-based mechanics. They can be composable—merged, split, or programmed. This is a profound shift. It makes ownership not merely a record, but a relationship. The NFT is not the end of the experience; it is often the beginning.

There is a sociological richness here. NFTs engage with our most primal desires—for recognition, for proof of participation, for uniqueness. The marketplace is a mirror, reflecting both our aspirations and our insecurities. Why does someone pay six figures for a digital penguin? Not for warmth or protection. For status, for access, for signalling taste in a language only some can decode. These are not irrational acts. They are deeply human ones, now expressed through cryptographic tools.

To navigate this space with intelligence requires a multidisciplinary lens. Financial analysis helps, yes—but so does anthropology, psychology, and design theory. Investors must understand not just blockchain mechanics, but meme cycles, influencer dynamics, and cultural semiotics. The value of an NFT is rarely embedded in its image; it lies in its context, narrative, and community traction. *Context is not just king—it's the entire kingdom.*

This chapter asks the reader to look beyond the price floor and into the cultural substratum of digital assets. What are these tokens *really* doing? Who are they empowering? What new forms of collective memory, economic infrastructure, or identity politics do they enable? And how might we shape this technology—rather than be shaped by it?

NFTs are trophies, yes. But they are also tests—of judgement, of timing, of imagination. To understand them as more than hype is to see them as artefacts of a shifting world, where ownership is public, programmable, and performative. And in that shift lies both extraordinary opportunity and unprecedented complexity.

Scarcity in Code: The Anatomy of Digital Value

Scarcity, in the traditional sense, is a function of limited supply relative to demand. It is anchored in the physical world—there are only so many beachfront properties, signed first editions, or Rembrandt paintings. Digital space, by contrast, appears boundless. Files are copied with keystrokes, streamed globally, duplicated infinitely. So how is scarcity—genuine, trustable, tradable scarcity—created in a medium designed for replication? The answer lies in code. In the architecture of blockchain protocols, in the integrity of smart contracts, and in the metadata that maps provenance to ownership, value in digital assets becomes not only possible, but programmable.

At the heart of this transformation is the concept of immutability. When a non-fungible token (NFT) is minted, it is logged on a blockchain—an open, append-only ledger that cannot be altered without consensus. This creates an unforgeable timestamp, which links the digital object to a specific moment, creator, and contract. That record becomes a certificate of authenticity, accessible to anyone, and validated by code rather than authority. *The blockchain becomes the museum wall, the legal deed, and the appraisal report all at once.*

Smart contracts take this further. They are self-executing scripts embedded into the blockchain, defining the rules under which digital assets behave. Who can sell it? What happens upon resale? What royalties are paid to the original creator? What metadata must be preserved? These contracts enforce scarcity by fixing quantity—an artist may code a maximum of 100 identical tokens, or 1 of 1—and ensuring that rules cannot be changed after deployment. This transforms trust: no intermediary, institution, or curator is needed to uphold the scarcity. It is embedded in the object itself.

This is critical. In traditional art or luxury goods, fakes undermine the market. Certificates can be forged, provenance faked, records lost. In the NFT context, metadata and smart contracts replace fallible paperwork with deterministic truth. Anyone can verify the origin, track the transaction history, and validate that a token is indeed part of a limited edition. *Rarity is not declared—it is enforced.*

Yet the creation of digital scarcity is not just technical. It is aesthetic, social, and psychological. Code makes scarcity possible; context makes it valuable. Consider two identical tokens with the same image. One is minted by a widely respected creator during the early days of a project. The other is minted later by a copycat. Both may be technically similar, but the former commands exponentially higher market value. Why? Because of provenance, reputation, and narrative. *Scarcity is not merely about quantity—it is about context, and context is encoded in culture.*

Take the example of the "Merge" by the pseudonymous digital artist Pak. Sold in December 2021, this NFT became one of the most expensive digital artworks ever sold, not because it was unique, but because it was structured as a dynamic, programmable mass. Buyers could purchase units of mass; the more units one held, the larger the final NFT. It was a demonstration of how code could manufacture both scarcity and abundance simultaneously—scarcity of final assets (consolidated into a single token per user) and abundance of access. *Smart contracts don't just enforce scarcity—they choreograph it.*

This choreography creates unique challenges in valuation. Traditional scarcity is visible: one sculpture, one canvas, one signature. Digital scarcity requires a new kind of literacy. The collector must understand not just what an NFT looks like, but how it was coded, under what terms, on what chain, by whom, and with what reputation. A failure in contract design—such as a mutable metadata link or centralised image hosting—can destroy trust instantly. *Scarcity is brittle when it relies on off-chain components or opaque design.*

Metadata integrity is often overlooked, but it is fundamental to digital value. The data associated with an NFT—its image, attributes, history, links—must remain accessible and immutable. If metadata is hosted on a centralised server that disappears or is hacked, the token becomes a shell. Its hash still exists on-chain, but the object it points to may not. This fragility has led to the rise of decentralised storage systems like IPFS (InterPlanetary File System) and Arweave, which aim to preserve the digital artefact beyond the lifespan of any single host. *Digital scarcity without metadata permanence is like a banknote with no backing—it loses its meaning.*

Scarcity in digital assets also has a performative component. Projects often manufacture demand by limiting supply—capping token numbers, gating access, or creating artificial scarcity through timed drops and auctions. This tactic, borrowed from streetwear and luxury goods, works because it leverages FOMO (fear of missing out) and mimetic desire. But there is a risk: if scarcity is perceived as manipulative or baseless, it undermines credibility. The most successful projects anchor scarcity in meaningful design, narrative coherence, or verifiable utility. *Manufactured scarcity must feel earned, not imposed.*

The speculative nature of digital assets further complicates the picture. When rarity becomes a proxy for investment potential, not cultural value, markets can spiral into hype cycles. Tokens are priced not for what they represent, but for what others might pay tomorrow. This erodes the role of scarcity as a quality signal. The challenge, then, is to balance technical scarcity with conceptual richness. NFTs that endure—like generative artworks from Art Blocks or culturally resonant projects like World of Women—succeed because they fuse scarcity with purpose. *Rarity is more than numbers—it is significance encoded in code.*

We must also confront the issue of copy-paste culture. In a medium where images and files are trivially replicable, many critics argue that NFTs are meaningless. "I can right-click and save the image," they say. But this misses the point. Just as owning a signed first edition differs from photocopying its pages, owning a tokenised object with on-chain provenance is about legal and social recognition, not file exclusivity. The NFT is not the image—it is the ledger entry, the contractual wrapper, the programmable identity. *It is scarcity transposed onto abundance.*

This transposition opens up new economic models. Think of fractional ownership, where a rare NFT is split into fungible tokens. Or burn mechanics, where users must destroy tokens to access new assets. These behaviours, governed by smart contracts, create scarcity through participation. They reward engagement and penalise inaction. The asset becomes alive—capable of changing, evolving, or disappearing, depending on how users interact with it. *Scarcity, in this context, is not static—it is gamified.*

The future of digital scarcity will hinge on standards and transparency. As more creators, institutions, and investors enter the space, the demand for auditability, interoperability, and archival integrity will grow. The ERC-721 and ERC-1155 standards on Ethereum already define how NFTs function, but further norms will be needed: metadata schemas, provenance registries, reputation systems. The more consistent and verifiable these layers become, the more robust the idea of digital rarity will be. *Code may create scarcity—but trust turns it into value.*

Ultimately, the anatomy of digital value is not found in pixels, file types, or even cryptographic hashes. It is found in the interplay between code, culture, and consensus. Scarcity is no longer a matter of what we cannot touch—it is a function of what we can verify. This changes not only how we invest, but how we understand ownership, art, and authenticity itself. In a world of infinite replication, rarity must be earned, engineered, and explained. And that makes it all the more powerful.

From JPEGs to Jurisdictions: Legal and Tax Implications

What does it mean to "own" something that cannot be physically possessed, that lives on a decentralised ledger, and may be viewed, copied, or shared by anyone at will? This question sits at the centre of NFT ownership, and the answer is neither simple nor fully resolved. NFTs—non-fungible tokens—purport to represent ownership of digital goods. But legal systems were not built to adjudicate possession by smart contract. The implications for property rights, intellectual ownership, and taxation are profound. As digital assets grow in economic significance, understanding their legal contours is not optional—it's foundational.

Let's begin with the core fallacy that haunts many new entrants to the NFT market: *owning an NFT does not necessarily mean owning the underlying content.* Buying an NFT linked to a digital image, video, or file typically grants ownership of the token itself—a unique identifier on a blockchain—but not the copyright, licensing rights, or commercial usage of the associated content unless explicitly stated. The NFT is metadata and provenance, not the image itself. Without clear terms coded into the smart contract or outlined in accompanying legal documents, the buyer often acquires little more than bragging rights and transactional history. *Legal ownership and digital possession are not synonymous.*

This ambiguity creates tension between technical certainty and legal vagueness. On the blockchain, the NFT is yours—it is cryptographically signed, timestamped, and verifiable. No one can modify or delete it without consensus. But in a court of law, the question becomes: what rights does this token confer? The answer varies by jurisdiction and is still in flux. In most cases, NFT ownership grants *proof of purchase*—not proof of authorship, not an automatic licence, and certainly not the ability to sue for infringement if someone else uses the associated media.

Consider the case of Quentin Tarantino's NFT project based on the original screenplay of *Pulp Fiction*. When Tarantino attempted to mint pages from the unpublished script as NFTs, Miramax, the film studio, sued—arguing that despite Tarantino's creative input, the rights to monetise derivative works belonged to the studio. The dispute underscored a central legal problem in the NFT space: *blockchain records do not override intellectual property contracts.* Artists, brands, and investors must understand the difference between minting and licensing. One is technical; the other is legal.

This divergence becomes even more pronounced when dealing with decentralised marketplaces. Platforms like OpenSea or Blur may host NFT listings, but they are not equivalent to traditional auction houses or art galleries. They rarely conduct due diligence on sellers, verify authenticity, or adjudicate ownership claims. This leaves the legal burden squarely on the buyer. If an NFT is minted without the creator's permission or misrepresents its rights, buyers may face litigation or loss of access. Unlike with physical goods, where ownership can be more intuitively tracked and enforced, digital assets require *vigilant scrutiny of provenance and permissions.*

Even storage introduces complications. While NFTs reside on-chain, the digital files they point to—images, animations, documents—often live off-chain, hosted on servers, IPFS, or cloud storage. This opens up questions of custodianship, continuity, and liability. If the hosting service disappears, the NFT may remain intact, but its perceived value can evaporate. Moreover, if that content is deemed defamatory, obscene, or infringing, legal authorities may take action against the server host, even though the token persists. *Digital permanence doesn't mean legal invincibility.*

Then there's the matter of jurisdiction. Blockchain technology is borderless by design, but legal systems are not. Where is an NFT "located"? Where is it taxed? If a Singapore-based investor purchases an NFT minted by a UK artist on a decentralised exchange headquartered nominally in the Cayman Islands, under which tax authority does the transaction fall? This is not just an academic question. Regulatory agencies worldwide—from the SEC in the US to the FCA in the UK—are scrambling to assert control over digital assets. And their answers differ.

In the United States, the IRS currently treats NFTs as property for tax purposes. This means that sales, trades, or even gifting of NFTs may trigger capital gains taxes. If you bought an NFT for £1,000 worth of ETH and sold it for £5,000 worth of ETH, you owe tax on the £4,000 gain—even if you never converted the ETH into fiat currency. Further complexity arises if the NFT was acquired with crypto that itself appreciated. Now you're calculating gains on two separate assets: the crypto and the NFT. *Digital asset taxation is not only a record-keeping nightmare—it is a compliance risk.*

The UK's HMRC echoes many of these principles. NFTs are subject to Capital Gains Tax when disposed of (including through sale or trade). Inheritance tax may also apply if NFTs are bequeathed. But defining fair market value for volatile, thinly traded assets is difficult. If an NFT sells for £50,000 today but is illiquid for months afterward, how do tax authorities evaluate its real worth? The lack of established benchmarks, pricing indices, and custody standards makes NFT taxation murky. Investors must be proactive, not reactive, in documenting transactions, valuations, and rights. *Tax authorities will not wait for legal clarity to pursue enforcement.*

Corporate and institutional actors face even more hurdles. For businesses purchasing NFTs—whether for investment, marketing, or intellectual property expansion—the accounting treatment remains unclear. Are NFTs intangible assets? Inventory? Financial instruments? Most current accounting standards do not explicitly address tokenised assets. This leads to inconsistent treatment across balance sheets, audits, and risk disclosures. As companies like Nike, Gucci, and Meta experiment with digital ownership, the pressure for regulatory guidance will intensify. *Until then, organisations must proceed with caution—and robust legal counsel.*

There's also the consumer protection dimension. With digital assets easily transferred, often pseudonymously, and subject to irreversible transactions, the potential for fraud is high. Rug pulls—where developers vanish after raising funds—are rampant. So are phishing scams, fake mint links, and metadata manipulations. When victims attempt to recover funds or prosecute bad actors, they often run into jurisdictional gridlock. Which court has standing? What laws apply? What if the seller is anonymous or the platform non-cooperative? The decentralised ethos that underpins Web3 innovation also fragments legal accountability. *Decentralisation without safeguards is not empowerment—it is exposure.*

Yet, despite these risks, digital assets are not outside the reach of regulation. Courts are adapting. In 2022, a UK court granted permission to serve legal documents via an NFT airdrop. Several jurisdictions have recognised NFTs as property in legal disputes. Intellectual property law firms now draft NFT licensing agreements that mirror those used in media and entertainment. Smart contracts are being designed to encode legal terms alongside code logic. The frontier is still uneven, but *the trend is toward convergence—code and law will increasingly speak to one another.*

This convergence will demand new skillsets. NFT creators must understand copyright, royalties, and moral rights. Investors must grasp tax implications, cross-border risks, and contract law. Developers must anticipate not just technical exploits, but regulatory scrutiny. Lawyers must learn to read smart contracts as legal instruments. The days of creative chaos are numbered; the future of digital ownership will be structured, enforceable, and litigated. *The question is no longer whether NFTs have legal consequences—it's whether you are prepared to navigate them.*

NFTs and digital assets are not exempt from the rule of law; they are testing its limits. As governments catch up, the regulatory frameworks will harden. This is not a reason to withdraw from the space—it is a call to engage with greater rigour. Those who understand the legal infrastructure underpinning digital value will be better equipped to participate in markets that are increasingly borderless, programmable, and real. You may buy a JPEG, but what you own—and owe—extends far beyond the screen.

The Speculation Singularity

When speculation becomes indistinguishable from belief, markets detach from reality. Nowhere is this more evident than in the recent rise of digital assets—particularly NFTs and Web3-related tokens—where investor enthusiasm often outpaces functional use, and price is frequently conflated with value. The result is a kind of speculative singularity: a feedback loop of hype, liquidity, and self-reinforcing narratives that blur the boundary between innovation and illusion. For the serious investor, the challenge is not whether to engage with emerging technologies, but how to do so with scepticism, discernment, and a robust framework for separating long-term promise from short-term noise.

At the heart of speculative fervour lies the seductive logic of "firsts." First token, first drop, first protocol, first mover—each becomes a marketing hook, not just a historical milestone. The market tends to reward perceived novelty with inflated valuations, creating an incentive to mint, launch, or issue before fully testing utility or governance. But history offers cautionary parallels. The dot-com era similarly elevated startups with minimal revenue but maximum buzz. Pets.com had a mascot; Theranos had a myth. The pattern persists in decentralised markets: *the faster something gains traction without utility, the more carefully one should interrogate its fundamentals.*

To understand where hype ends and risk begins, it helps to distinguish between technological viability and market euphoria. Blockchain, decentralised finance, and programmable assets are indeed important innovations. But so were subprime mortgages and synthetic credit derivatives—until they were leveraged into collapse. A technology's capability does not guarantee its profitable application. NFTs may represent the future of digital property rights, but that doesn't mean every profile picture or cartoon animal token carries investment merit. *Speculation occurs not when people believe in the future, but when they stop questioning which futures are plausible.*

The psychological dynamics of speculation are well-studied but still underappreciated in new asset classes. Scarcity, social proof, and FOMO (fear of missing out) act as accelerants, especially in online communities where financial discourse is infused with tribalism. The influence of Discord groups, Twitter influencers, and anonymous founders can quickly turn subjective enthusiasm into perceived consensus. In such an environment, due diligence is often replaced by meme velocity. *Conviction, when untethered from analysis, becomes collective self-hypnosis.*

What further complicates digital speculation is the illusion of liquidity. On decentralised exchanges and NFT marketplaces, the ease of listing, buying, and trading gives the impression of active demand. But thin markets and wash trading practices (where entities trade with themselves to simulate activity) often distort true value. The $1.5 million NFT sale may have been between wallets controlled by the same party. Without verifiable buyer diversity and organic price discovery, price signals become noise. Worse, they become bait. *Liquidity is not just a feature of markets—it is a test of whether interest can be sustained once hype fades.*

Compounding these risks is the gamification of investing. When platforms use loot box mechanics, leaderboards, rewards for referrals, or badge-based status, they borrow from the psychology of addiction more than the discipline of capital allocation. The investor is transformed into a player, and the asset into a token of participation, not value. This is not unique to crypto. Robinhood's stock trading interface or Reddit's meme stock campaigns reflect similar dynamics. But in digital assets, where the line between entertainment and investment is razor-thin, *the danger lies in mistaking engagement for understanding.*

Some proponents argue that early speculation is the price of innovation—that bubbles are necessary to fund breakthroughs, build infrastructure, and discover what sticks. There is some truth in this. The internet's backbone was built on the ashes of many failed dot-coms. But speculation only proves productive if it leaves behind durable value. The Ethereum network, for instance, emerged from the ashes of ICO hype as a platform with measurable utility. By contrast, projects that collapse entirely or were never designed to function beyond their tokenomics leave little more than digital debris. *The test of a speculative cycle is not how high it goes—but what survives after it crashes.*

Disciplined investors in this space ask questions that resist euphoria: Who is the team behind the project, and what is their track record? What problem does the token solve, and why is a blockchain necessary for its solution? Are tokenomics designed for sustainability or extraction? How is governance handled? Are users aligned with long-term value creation or merely incentivised to pump and exit? What are the barriers to replication or forks? Without such scrutiny, enthusiasm becomes indistinguishable from naiveté. *Scepticism is not cynicism—it is the scaffolding of intelligent risk.*

This is not to dismiss all activity as hype. There are genuine breakthroughs happening in digital identity, creator monetisation, decentralised coordination, and immutable provenance. But none of these require valuations untethered from reality. The test of a good investment is not whether it participates in a trend, but whether it endures beyond it. Investors must be willing to bypass the noise of Twitter feeds, bypass the dopamine of overnight multiples, and commit to deeper research. In a field driven by speed, patience is contrarian—and therefore powerful.

One must also consider time horizons. Speculation operates on the clock of minutes and hours. Innovation works on the scale of years. The two are not always compatible. If a technology is truly transformative, its impact may not be immediately reflected in price. Conversely, if price movements are the only indicator of worth, then the underlying technology is irrelevant to the thesis. Smart capital understands this and calibrates accordingly. Traders may profit from volatility, but investors seek compounded relevance. *The question is not whether something will go up—but whether it will matter five years from now.*

Finally, there is a broader ethical consideration. When speculation dominates, it reshapes not only markets but mindsets. Projects prioritise marketing over engineering. Builders chase liquidity rather than product-market fit. Newcomers are drawn not by vision, but by volatility. This is not sustainable. For the digital asset ecosystem to mature, it must wean itself off speculative excess and reward long-term thinking. This includes designing tokenomics that incentivise value creation, not quick exits; building governance structures that resist manipulation; and promoting education that goes beyond price charts and jargon. *If Web3 is to become more than a casino with better branding, it must graduate from speculation to significance.*

The speculative singularity is not inevitable. It is a choice—one made daily by investors, developers, influencers, and platforms. By interrogating narratives, demanding evidence, and privileging substance over spectacle, participants can shape a digital economy that is not only profitable but principled. The alternative is a cycle of booms and busts, where every lesson must be re-learned, and every promise delayed. The tools for progress exist. What remains is the discipline to use them well.

Chapter 9
Scams, Schemes, and Sophistication

The fascination with alternative investments stems from their promise: outsized returns, diversification unlinked to conventional markets, and the allure of discovering hidden value. Yet these same qualities that entice also harbour peril. Complexity, novelty, and limited oversight—hallmarks of alternative assets—create fertile ground for deception. Fraud is hardly new, but its most inventive forms often appear at the fringes, where innovation outpaces regulation and enthusiasm dulls caution. At the heart of alternative investing lies a tension that cannot be ignored: the delicate balance between curiosity and caution, between pioneering opportunity and predatory manipulation.

Many assume fraud is easy to spot: implausible returns, an elusive promoter, sudden disappearance. Reality is far subtler. Today's scams are often meticulously dressed in sophistication. Sleek branding, tech pedigree, and polished whitepapers lend an air of legitimacy. Buzzwords—blockchain, AI, ESG, fractionalisation—become siren calls rather than descriptors. Distinguishing a legitimate fund from a Ponzi scheme requires more than intuition; it demands understanding the mechanics, the verifiable architecture underpinning the venture. Ignorance here is not bliss—it is liability.

Alternative assets thrive on ambiguity. A whisky cask's value hinges on age and storage conditions; a rare sneaker's price fluctuates with cultural taste; a parcel of land can rise or fall with geopolitics. Such variables present genuine opportunity, but also ample room for obfuscation. In the absence of standardised financial disclosures, due diligence becomes detective work. Investors evaluate not just assets but narratives—and some narratives are crafted with deliberate intent to mislead.

This chapter begins by tracing how fraud has evolved across unconventional markets. From Renaissance art forgeries to modern DeFi rug pulls, the lessons are clear: the tools may change, but human psychology remains remarkably constant. Greed, urgency, social proof, and the seduction of complexity are the levers. The most sophisticated frauds are those that flatter the intelligence of their target, making the deception almost irresistible.

The aesthetic dimension of allure also warrants scrutiny. Some investments attract capital not through promise of return, but by projecting exclusivity, rarity, or visionary appeal. This is performative theatre. A private jet fractional ownership or a carbon credit token endorsed by a former diplomat may appear credible precisely because it aligns with aspiration. Presentation substitutes for transparency, and the discerning investor must remain alert.

Next, we examine a practical framework for spotting red flags before they metastasise into loss. This is not paranoia; it is pattern recognition. Does the structure resist independent verification? Are fees hidden, excessive, or asymmetric? Is custodial control centralised and opaque? Is liquidity real, or artificially engineered? These questions help distinguish legitimate complexity from obfuscation. Skepticism, far from being an obstacle, functions as a safeguard for innovation.

Yet vigilance need not calcify into cynicism. Sophisticated investing is less about possessing all the answers than about knowing which questions matter. It requires humility, the willingness to revisit assumptions, interrogate consensus, and pause when speed becomes the sales tactic. Risk is not merely numerical; it is narrative. The most capable investors are those aware of their own susceptibility to deception.

As alternative markets expand—propelled by technological breakthroughs, demographic shifts, and the pursuit of yield—so too will the ingenuity of fraudsters. But investors can evolve in parallel. Equipped with sharper tools, deeper awareness, and disciplined inquiry, one can navigate these complex arenas successfully. This chapter aims to arm the reader not simply to recognise pitfalls, but to operate confidently amidst them: with clarity, rigorous questioning, and a mindset primed for alert engagement. Preparedness, not paranoia, distinguishes the truly sophisticated investor.

Fraud in the Fringe

The margins of finance have always offered a curious contradiction: they promise both the most transformative opportunities and the most inventive betrayals. It is precisely this ambiguity—where innovation blurs into ambiguity, and regulation lags behind ambition—that makes alternative markets such fertile ground for financial deceit. Whether cloaked in the prestige of fine art, the science of synthetic biology, or the novelty of digital tokens, fraud thrives where traditional oversight thins out and the promise of asymmetric returns suspends critical scrutiny. *In these liminal zones, fraud is not an anomaly—it is a feature masquerading as a footnote.*

The myth that fraud is largely a problem of the unsophisticated or the ill-informed is not only dangerous—it is incorrect. Some of the most enduring scams have targeted educated professionals, lured not by naivety but by narrative. The smarter the investor, the more complex the deception must become. That complexity often wears the clothing of credibility: legal structures, detailed slide decks, a tokenised asset paired with jargon-heavy disclosures. The con evolves with its quarry. Today's fraud is not run by grifters in smoky backrooms—it's delivered via webinars, distributed on venture-capital-backed platforms, and sometimes lauded in mainstream press before unravelling under scrutiny.

Historical examples remind us that the shape of a scam is almost never static. In the 1980s, the fine wine market saw a rise in counterfeit bottles—fakes so convincing they fooled connoisseurs and auction houses alike. One infamous case involved collector Rudy Kurniawan, who manufactured rare vintages in his California kitchen, complete with forged labels and fabricated provenance. The deception wasn't just about taste—it was about trust in the system: the paperwork, the brand names, the social proof. Investors weren't buying wine; they were buying a story of prestige. That story collapsed spectacularly, not because it lacked detail, but because it lacked verification.

The same dynamic persists today, albeit with new technologies and narratives. In the cryptocurrency space, "rug pulls" have become a modern case study in opportunistic fraud. In such schemes, developers raise capital by selling tokens tied to ambitious-sounding decentralised projects. Once enough capital is pooled, the creators vanish—often within days—leaving behind worthless code and investor despair. These schemes do not rely on unsophisticated victims. On the contrary, many attract early-stage tech investors who fancy themselves trendspotters. *The speed of deception has accelerated, but its underlying psychology remains ancient: bait the desire to be early, elite, and above the herd.*

Fraud in the alternative market sphere also exploits regulatory ambiguity. Grey zones are not gaps in oversight—they are active zones of play. In real estate tokenisation, for instance, assets can be structured in such a way that they technically avoid registration with securities regulators, even while acting functionally as investment vehicles. Some promoters use this structure deliberately, dancing just outside the jurisdiction of accountability. The ethical problem isn't just non-disclosure—it's anti-disclosure. When complexity becomes the moat, transparency becomes the casualty.

And yet, the most powerful scams don't need to break the law. Many thrive within it. Consider multi-level marketing schemes that operate under the veneer of legality but produce economic outcomes strikingly similar to pyramid schemes. When marketed through the language of entrepreneurship and personal freedom, these systems become difficult to challenge without appearing paternalistic. The framing is clever: regulators look like overreaching bureaucrats, while the fraudsters appear as misunderstood innovators. *It's not illegality that defines a scam—it's the asymmetry of information and outcome, the predictable misalignment between pitch and performance.*

Alternative asset classes like rare sneakers, sports cards, NFTs, or pre-IPO equity are particularly susceptible to fraud due to their inherent opacity. Pricing is often illiquid and subjective, dependent on social consensus rather than cash flow or asset backing. These markets also attract new entrants—many of them financially literate but contextually inexperienced—who mistake familiarity with risk. In these spaces, influence often replaces insight. When a notable figure "apes in" to a new asset, the herd follows, assuming the presence of smart money. The reality is often more cynical: the influencer was paid in tokens, cashed out early, and left their audience holding the risk.

Such strategies extend beyond digital assets. In the fine art world, provenance fraud is a centuries-old phenomenon. Today, that fraud may involve digital certificates, tampered databases, or collusion among dealers. Even in timberland or farmland investments—seemingly tangible and safe—fraud can appear in the form of overstated yields, forged environmental credentials, or phantom properties listed in opaque jurisdictions. The veneer of ESG legitimacy often disarms even the most seasoned investor. Greenwashing, in this context, becomes a tool not merely for reputational gain, but for financial extraction. *When ethics become a marketing strategy, trust becomes a liability.*

To combat fraud in these fringe domains, vigilance must evolve into a framework. Verification cannot be retroactive—it must be designed into the investment process. That means demanding transparency not just from people, but from systems: asking whether platforms have audited smart contracts, whether third-party custody exists, whether legal recourse is enforceable across borders. It means looking past hype cycles and reputational halo to examine actual mechanics. And it means developing a muscle most investors under-train: the willingness to walk away when something looks promising but unverifiable.

Curiously, fraud often flourishes where the most potential lies. This is the paradox of the fringe: the frontier and the fraudster occupy the same geography. Real innovation will always attract opportunists. That is not a reason to retreat from alternatives—it is a reason to approach them with both curiosity and constraint. The best investors don't just evaluate opportunities; they interrogate them. They ask not just, "What's the upside?" but "Where is the mechanism of failure?" They understand that due diligence is not a checklist—it is a mindset. *And in alternative markets, that mindset is not merely prudent; it is protective.*

Understanding fraud is not about becoming a cynic. It is about becoming an operator who can recognise the boundary between risk and ruin. In a landscape where novelty often disguises vulnerability, the most valuable skill is neither technical fluency nor insider access—it is the disciplined habit of asking difficult questions, early and often. This chapter offers that discipline. The frauds will continue to evolve. But so, too, can the investor.

If It Sounds Sexy, It Might Be Dangerous

The more seductive an investment pitch, the more critical your scepticism should become. The alternative asset landscape, rich with innovation and ambition, has also become a playground for narratives that appeal to emotion over analysis. From luxury whiskey casks and speculative NFTs to fractional ownership of exotic racehorses or rare sneakers, the language of investment has absorbed the vocabulary of desire. Scarcity, exclusivity, disruption, and access—these are no longer merely marketing buzzwords. They have become emotional triggers, capable of blinding even seasoned investors to fundamental due diligence.

One of the most dangerous qualities of "sexy" investments is their ability to masquerade as rational decisions while riding on waves of novelty, prestige, or social signalling. Investment in a startup launching a rare gemstone-backed cryptocurrency sounds edgy, tech-forward, and elite. But beneath that aesthetic veneer, how many such ventures have robust governance structures, liquidity pathways, or audited reserves? The danger is not that these ideas are inherently flawed—but that their allure can create an analytical blind spot precisely where caution is most warranted.

Psychological studies have long noted the effects of the "halo bias," where our perception of one impressive attribute leads us to assume overall quality. A well-designed website, an articulate founder, or a flashy investor deck can generate trust before the underlying fundamentals are examined. Nowhere is this truer than in markets that trade on appearance or cultural capital. Consider a case where an emerging artist's digital NFT collection is released in tandem with a luxury fashion house collaboration. The market responds not to the quality or durability of the asset, but to the symbolic associations it conjures. Risk is camouflaged beneath aesthetic appeal.

It's easy to scoff at retail investors who poured savings into celebrity-endorsed tokens or speculative metaverse land grabs. But many of these same misjudgements play out in more "respectable" contexts as well. A prime vineyard parcel, marketed to investors via a glossy brochure detailing terroir, winemaking heritage, and global demand growth, may appear foolproof. Yet if the land lacks appropriate irrigation rights, if yields are falling due to climate change, or if local regulations impede resale, these hidden frictions can erode anticipated returns. The more beautiful the story, the more brutal the facts must be.

Allure has also infiltrated the language of access. Investment opportunities framed as "previously unavailable to the public" or "reserved for institutional insiders" activate a potent emotional lever: the fear of missing out. The packaging of exclusivity adds a layer of urgency to an already compelling narrative. But sophisticated investors must invert this logic. Scarcity alone is not value. A closed door is not always hiding treasure. And access is meaningless if it leads to an underperforming or opaque asset. True access should be defined by informational transparency, not exclusivity posturing.

To resist the seduction of style over substance, a few fundamental heuristics become invaluable. The first is to disaggregate the aesthetic from the economic. Ask: If this product were stripped of its visual packaging, influencer endorsements, or cultural associations, would the numbers still justify the price? Would the asset's utility, demand dynamics, and exit pathway still hold water? The best test of investment soundness is often how it performs under an unembellished lens.

Second, evaluate the role of story in the pitch. Stories are powerful. They create narrative coherence in uncertain markets. But they can also distract from inconvenient truths. The danger is not storytelling itself—it's storytelling in place of substance. Every compelling narrative should be backed by verifiable data, independent valuations, and legal clarity. The more elaborate the backstory, the more disciplined your fact-checking should be.

A third principle is *dispassionate inversion*: the art of thinking through the downside before entertaining the upside. When presented with a new alternative asset, invert the proposal. What are the most likely failure points? What assumptions must hold true for the investment thesis to work? Is the path to liquidity clear or contingent on speculative future interest? This inversion flips the framing from seduction to stress testing—an essential mindset in emotionally charged markets.

Consider the case of exotic car funds, which pool investor capital to acquire and manage rare vehicles with anticipated capital appreciation. The concept is glamorous, steeped in nostalgia, and backed by a handful of spectacular sale records at elite auctions. But under scrutiny, questions emerge. Are maintenance costs and storage fully accounted for? What are the risks of depreciation from usage or environmental wear? Who is the end buyer, and what drives resale velocity? The returns may be real, but they are far from automatic.

This kind of critical interrogation is especially urgent in early-stage technologies and Web3 assets. The aesthetics of decentralisation, community-driven governance, and tokenised economies often overshadow the messy legal, regulatory, and operational details underneath. Many token projects, for instance, promise high yields through liquidity mining or staking—but obscure the source of those yields, the tokenomics of inflation, or the lock-in risks. Complexity is often presented as innovation, when it may in fact be obfuscation.

Even well-intentioned projects can suffer from over-hyped narratives. Impact investing platforms offering carbon credits, regenerative agriculture tokens, or digital art designed to support indigenous communities may carry noble aims. But if the underlying market mechanics are poorly structured, if verification protocols are weak, or if exit options are unclear, the ethical narrative can't compensate for commercial fragility. One must be wary of confusing emotional alignment with financial rigour.

To sharpen dispassionate clarity, sophisticated investors are learning to ask harder questions—and to ask them earlier. Is there third-party verification of the asset's valuation? Are the incentives of the platform aligned with the investor, or with volume-based fees? Is the custody of the asset—be it physical or digital—legally enforceable? Is the offering jurisdictionally regulated, and if so, by whom? These questions may not make headlines, but they are what separate signal from noise.

This vigilance also applies to the self. One must ask: Why am I drawn to this deal? Is it because the return profile is superior, or because the idea makes me feel early, special, or clever? The need for self-interrogation grows in proportion to the allure of the investment. Emotional attraction is not inherently disqualifying—but it demands a doubling of analytical discipline.

In financial circles, the phrase "too good to be true" is often repeated but rarely internalised. The truth is, if an opportunity feels thrilling before it has been fully understood, it warrants the most caution. Real alpha rarely arrives in neon. It usually comes dressed in patience, complexity, and a degree of discomfort. Sexy deals are easy to sell. Sound ones take work to understand. The wise investor learns to resist the shortcut of seduction and embrace the rigor of clarity. That discipline is not just protective—it's profitable.

Spotting the Red Flags: A Field Guide for Scam Detection in Alternative Assets

Scams flourish in opacity, and alternative investments—by their very nature—tend to dwell in the shadows of traditional finance. Where regulation is light, market norms are still forming, and investor excitement outpaces comprehension, deceit finds oxygen. Sophisticated frauds no longer rely on crude trickery; they embed themselves in language, structure, and hype. The aim of this guide is not merely to sound alarms, but to sharpen perception—so that discernment becomes a default, not a defensive reflex.

A compelling alternative asset pitch often mimics the architecture of credibility. There is usually a story of scarcity, an influencer endorsement, and the intoxicating aroma of being early. But underneath can lie one of several recurring patterns: unregistered securities disguised as exclusive deals, manufactured provenance, falsified yields, or vehicles designed more to extract fees than to deliver returns. Dissecting these signals requires not just technical knowledge but a temperament of quiet scepticism—especially when the promise feels effortlessly appealing.

Unregistered offerings are perhaps the most common gateway to financial injury in alternative markets. Promoters will tout access to pre-IPO shares, rare commodities, or insider allocations, accompanied by legalese that suggests exemption from oversight. What they omit is that exemptions under securities law (like Regulation D or crowdfunding carve-outs) come with clear disclosure obligations. If the offering is pitched as "private," "pre-regulated," or "off-market," yet lacks a clear filing reference, investor protections are likely absent—and so is recourse if things unravel. Sophisticated scams cloak themselves in the trappings of regulation while sidestepping its actual substance.

False scarcity is another hallmark. Limited editions, closed series, or time-sensitive tokens can instil artificial urgency. But in the digital economy, scarcity is a choice, not a constraint. NFTs, for instance, can be minted infinitely unless coded otherwise. Physical assets like wine or art can be replicated or counterfeited, especially when authentication chains are loose. Smart investors don't just ask *whether* something is rare—they ask *why*, *how verified*, and *by whom*. Provenance, chain of custody, and third-party audits should not be optional—they are structural necessities. Scarcity without substantiation is theatre, not finance.

When high returns are paired with low transparency, caution becomes compulsory. If an investment offers double-digit yields but refuses to share its methodology, underlying assets, or risk modelling, that opacity is not a feature—it's a red flag. This holds especially true for alternative funds that aggregate capital across crypto, collectibles, or emerging markets. Is the fund externally audited? Are the GP/LP incentives aligned? Are performance fees charged on realised gains, or on paper marks? Transparency in structure must match the transparency of the asset itself—or else the vehicle becomes the vulnerability.

Ponzi-like dynamics continue to mutate across asset classes. A new tactic involves fractionalised ownership platforms, where demand for the asset is sustained not by its intrinsic value, but by an ever-expanding base of users who buy into a narrative. Watch for products that promise liquidity through internal resale markets but lack sufficient third-party demand. Platforms that guarantee exit windows without external bidders are essentially running liquidity loops that resemble pyramid logic. Markets built on momentum, not fundamentals, can quickly reverse when enthusiasm cools.

Another signal of concern is language that overcompensates. Any offer that leans heavily on branding, emotion, or celebrity endorsement deserves forensic attention. In traditional finance, pedigree is established through audit trails, regulatory filings, and third-party evaluation. In the alternative space, branding often attempts to substitute for these. Slick decks, aggressive copywriting, and terms like "revolutionary," "disruptive," or "elite" are designed to pre-empt your critical instincts. The more an investment appeals to ego or exclusivity, the more it demands verification.

Legal structure is another overlooked dimension. Many alternative assets are held through special purpose vehicles (SPVs), trusts, or pooled investment entities. The devil is often in the details. What jurisdiction governs the entity? Who controls the bank accounts? Can the investor vote, redeem, or exit under defined conditions—or are rights entirely discretionary? Complex legal wrappers are sometimes used not for tax optimisation but for obfuscation. Investors must examine term sheets, not just whitepapers. If rights and remedies are buried or ambiguous, that's not innovation—it's insulation from liability.

Fees, when structured aggressively, can quietly erode even strong gross returns. Especially in esoteric assets—like music royalties, carbon credits, or metaverse land—fee layers may be nested and hard to isolate. Look for retroactive performance fees, hidden marketing costs, or operational fees indexed to assets under management rather than actual revenue. Always ask: Who profits even if the asset underperforms? Misalignment of incentives between managers and investors is not just a business flaw—it's a philosophical breach.

One of the subtlest but most damaging red flags is excessive simplicity in complex markets. If a pitch reduces a multi-variable investment—say, distressed timberland, or a tokenised art fund—into a one-line narrative like "inflation hedge" or "next Bitcoin," scepticism should spike. Real assets are messy, subject to market cycles, policy shifts, and geopolitical risk. Anyone selling frictionless upside is either naive or deceptive. The right response is not cynicism, but precision: ask for assumptions, ask for scenarios, ask for stress testing.

History provides ample warning. From the early 2000s wine pyramid schemes in Europe to contemporary crypto rug pulls, fraud tends to evolve faster than regulation. And unlike equity markets, which benefit from central clearing, robust custody, and standardised disclosures, many alternative investments are fragmented and borderless. This makes them fertile ground for cross-jurisdictional evasion, where legal accountability becomes nearly impossible. Sophisticated frauds don't just take money—they weaponise complexity and investor fatigue.

The antidote to these threats is not paralysis, but education. No single checklist guarantees safety, but patterns emerge with experience. Learn to interrogate what isn't said. Study the pedigree of platforms and their founders. Be wary of opacity sold as exclusivity. Examine whether risks are acknowledged, or papered over with narrative. If a due diligence request is met with irritation, deflection, or urgency, that's not just impolite—that's informative.

Scam resistance isn't a fixed skill; it's a practice. It requires continuous recalibration as markets evolve. Above all, it requires investors to adopt what the best fraud investigators rely on: a blend of empathy and rigour. Empathy, to understand why people get seduced. Rigour, to test what lies behind the seduction. In alternative markets, where the boundary between vision and vaporware is often razor-thin, vigilance is not optional—it is foundational.

Staying Curious, Not Reckless

Among the most underestimated traits in modern investing—particularly within alternative assets—is restraint. Not the passive kind born of fear or inertia, but the active, engaged discipline of a curious mind that doesn't leap at the first shimmer of novelty. This form of intellectual humility, the ability to investigate without attachment and to explore without bias, becomes indispensable when navigating terrain that is, by design, unregulated, opaque, or newly emerging. In markets where metrics are ambiguous and narratives are seductive, curiosity must be paired with scepticism, not clouded by it.

Alternative asset markets—from tokenised art to regenerative timberland—operate in zones where conventional guardrails are either absent or evolving. Traditional due diligence frameworks are not always applicable. Valuations may be influenced by cultural hype, influencer endorsement, or speculative zeal rather than underlying utility or intrinsic worth. For those unaccustomed to operating without institutional scaffolding, this lack of clarity can trigger a false confidence—a belief that intuition, gut feeling, or social proof can replace analytical rigour. But *knowing that you don't know* is not a sign of weakness in these domains; it is the most effective risk control mechanism at your disposal.

The most dangerous investors in alternative markets are not the uninformed, but the half-informed—the ones who have read enough headlines to speak the language, but not enough white papers to understand the protocol. They can quote floor prices, but not token standards. They reference the soil quality of a parcel without understanding the liquidity constraints of agricultural real estate. In complex, thinly regulated environments, it is intellectual modesty—not bravado—that keeps capital safe. A seasoned investor will often ask, "What don't I see here?" before asking, "How can I benefit from this?"

This principle becomes particularly relevant when novelty is positioned as value. Newness in and of itself is not a virtue, though in alternative investing it is often marketed as such. Consider digital collectibles or virtual land: the early adopters are rewarded, not necessarily because the asset is sound, but because the narrative velocity temporarily outpaces scrutiny. When critical questioning is deferred in favour of FOMO-driven participation, the line between pioneering and gambling becomes perilously thin. Curiosity alone is not enough—it must be paired with a structured process of critical inquiry. What are the real revenue streams? Who controls access and resale rights? What happens if the platform disappears?

A further danger lies in equating access with understanding. Alternative investment platforms—especially those aimed at retail audiences—increasingly use sleek user interfaces and simplified language to lower the barrier to entry. While this democratises exposure, it can also dull scepticism. When a vintage wine fund promises double-digit returns through tokenised barrels or a crypto startup claims to fractionalise Picasso canvases on-chain, the accessibility masks the underlying complexity. It is deceptively easy to feel well-informed when, in fact, one is simply well-exposed. *Convenient participation is not the same as competent participation.*

Moreover, many alternative assets require the investor to be more than just a capital provider—they demand that one becomes a temporary custodian, analyst, or even evangelist. Whether you're acquiring early-stage music royalties or investing in decarbonised land use, your involvement extends into domains where knowledge is fragmented and oversight is thin. In such ecosystems, expertise is often decentralised. There is no single source of truth, only scattered data points, biased actors, and evolving interpretations. Staying curious here means building a mosaic from incomplete tiles, and resisting the urge to declare the picture finished.

Another challenge arises in how we benchmark success. In public equities or bonds, returns are standardised, comparisons are easy, and liquidity is near-instant. With NFTs, carbon credits, or vintage wristwatches, benchmarking becomes subjective. The temptation, then, is to seek validation through appreciation alone, regardless of the underlying logic. But a rising price does not validate the asset's long-term viability—it merely reflects temporary consensus. Without a grounded framework for evaluation, curiosity devolves into confirmation bias. A sophisticated investor must be able to separate the social energy of a market from the structural integrity of its assets.

Still, intellectual humility doesn't mean paralysis. The goal isn't to wait for perfect clarity—it's to build resilience in the face of ambiguity. In fact, the most effective investors in these spaces are those who treat each investment as a live hypothesis. They maintain open feedback loops. They are willing to be wrong early, correct swiftly, and learn publicly. This adaptive mindset transforms curiosity from a passive trait into an active strategy. Questions like "What am I missing?", "What are my incentives?", and "Who benefits if I believe this?" become part of the investor's core toolkit.

There's also a psychological dimension worth addressing: ego and identity. In many alternative markets—especially those that merge cultural capital with financial capital—investments become personal. To own a rare digital collectible, a regenerative farm share, or a founder's stake in a niche platform is to affiliate oneself with a certain ethos, movement, or ideology. This identification can make it difficult to disengage or reassess when the facts change. Intellectual humility requires a separation between what we own and who we are. Our portfolios should not reflect our self-worth, and we must retain the capacity to divest with the same clarity that led us to invest.

Consider, for example, the allure of sustainability-linked assets. A buyer might invest in forest carbon offsets or impact bonds not only for financial gain but because the asset aligns with their values. While alignment is admirable, it should not cloud evaluation. Not all ESG-labelled assets deliver what they promise, and many are riddled with greenwashing, poorly defined metrics, or vague accountability structures. Curiosity here requires not just belief in the cause, but a persistent probing of whether the execution matches the intention.

Likewise, community-driven projects—particularly common in Web3 environments—often blur the boundary between collaboration and cultism. While decentralised governance and crowd validation are intriguing mechanisms, they can also create echo chambers where scepticism is punished. Staying curious in these spaces means being willing to ask hard questions even when the social incentives discourage it. Are decisions really decentralised, or is power simply redistributed among the early and vocal? Is token distribution fair, or does it entrench inequality under the banner of openness?

Ultimately, curiosity is not just about acquiring knowledge—it's about building mental models that tolerate ambiguity. In opaque markets, you will often operate with partial information, conflicting data, and narrative volatility. The antidote is not certainty, but calibration. A good investor calibrates their conviction, adapts their exposure, and maintains a spectrum of mental outcomes. They can be optimistic without being naive, enthusiastic without being credulous, and sceptical without being cynical.

There's a final, unglamorous truth: in many cases, the best decision you'll make is to *not* invest. This restraint isn't lauded, and it won't be reflected in your portfolio dashboard, but it is one of the most powerful forms of sophistication. Knowing when *not* to act is what separates the professional from the opportunist. It is curiosity sharpened by caution, and it might just be the only competitive advantage that endures in a world where narratives move faster than fundamentals.

To remain an effective participant in alternative markets, cultivate a mindset that questions the obvious, resists easy consensus, and prizes truth over trend. The markets will always evolve. Scams will resurface in new clothes. Promises will outpace infrastructure. But a curious, dispassionate, and rigorously humble investor will not be easily seduced, nor easily deceived. They will adapt, absorb, and grow—without ever needing to gamble recklessly to stay ahead.

Chapter 10
The Wealth of Meaning

A portfolio is far more than a ledger of numbers; it is, in effect, a biography inscribed in capital. Every acquisition, divestment, and omission reveals underlying priorities, anxieties, and ambitions. Across the asset classes explored in this book, it becomes evident that investing is no longer purely quantitative; it is profoundly expressive. At a certain level of sophistication, the numerical and the philosophical entwine inseparably. This chapter begins where most guides conclude—by probing not what you own, but why.

In markets defined by volatility and shifting paradigms, returns fluctuate, yet meaning endures. The expansion of alternative investments offers not just profit but the opportunity to embed intention within a portfolio. This is no mere sentimental overlay; it is strategy. Investors aligned with their values tend to navigate storms more resiliently than those swayed by fashion or consensus. Such alignment—between principles and holdings—emerges as an increasingly rare form of alpha.

We inhabit an era saturated with financial tools, platforms, and narratives. Tokenised assets can be acquired in moments; rare artefacts change hands through rapid online auctions; ESG funds promise alignment between capital and conscience. Yet abundance breeds confusion. Curation has become as critical as access. The question has shifted from "Can I invest in this?" to "Should I?" Answering it demands more than due diligence; it requires discernment. Not moralising, but philosophical precision. What kind of world are you shaping with your capital? And who are you becoming through that construction?

Ownership itself is being reconsidered. In some contexts, it implies economic control; in others, it carries symbolic resonance. A collector may hold a rare piece of street art not for sale but to preserve culture. A family may retain ancestral land, not for yield, but for continuity. These are not merely assets; they are artefacts, accumulating narrative as well as value. Their significance often outlives any market cycle. In such cases, investment decisions resemble acts of stewardship rather than speculation.

Stewardship lies at the heart of this chapter. It counters the consumerist reflex that treats capital as fuel for personal gratification or abstract growth. Stewardship embodies responsibility, patience, and care. The investor becomes a custodian of meaning rather than a hunter of yield. This mindset resists outsourcing decisions to algorithms, institutions, or trends. It acknowledges that the most demanding and rewarding investments are those resistant to automation, where fewer positions, slower deliberation, and deeper convictions prevail.

This perspective naturally extends to intergenerational thinking. Assets can signal values across time, becoming touchstones that carry stories and lessons. Farms, books, watches, or shares in purpose-driven companies often outlive their owners, transmitting narrative resilience across generations. To see capital as a conduit for cultural inheritance is to operate on a timescale beyond the news cycle, privileging endurance over immediacy.

Yet meaning is not sentimentality. Emotionally charged assets are not automatically worth retaining, and cause-driven investments are not inherently prudent. Meaning, like alpha, requires calibration. This chapter provides frameworks to distinguish authenticity from affectation, alignment from indulgence. We explore how personalised investing tools—from direct indexing to thematic curation—enable portfolios to express individuality, though tools alone cannot imbue meaning; that remains the investor's responsibility.

Throughout, we examine how values-driven portfolios are realised in practice. We consider the interplay of art and permanence, land and legacy, sustainability and stewardship. Some investors approach collectibles not as trophies but as talismans; others retreat from markets to embrace less liquid but more resonant holdings. We interrogate mainstream assumptions: that liquidity is always virtuous, diversification paramount, risk primarily statistical. In place of these conventions, alternative logics emerge—those that account for identity, belief, memory, and belonging.

Ultimately, this chapter is not prescriptive. It will not dictate which assets are meaningful. That task remains yours. Its purpose is to sharpen the questions you ask: What does this asset communicate to my future self? Whose values does it reinforce? What am I endorsing by holding it? If passed forward, what would it teach? These inquiries are not abstract; they lie at the heart of financial life in a time when ownership is abundant, attention scarce, and meaning the ultimate rarity.

By the chapter's end, readers should possess not only a clearer understanding of what their portfolio reveals about them but also a more deliberate sense of what they wish it to convey. Wealth of meaning resides not in returns alone, but in alignment, story, and stewardship. In a world awash with volatility and distraction, a portfolio that embodies one's clearest convictions may be the rarest—and most valuable—asset of all.

Your Portfolio is a Mirror

Every investment is a decision, but not every decision is examined. Investors often speak of portfolios as if they were mechanical constructs—tools for wealth generation, diversified bundles of risk, or exposure to asset classes. Rarely are they spoken of as personal artefacts. But they are. Portfolios, whether curated with precision or assembled through inertia, are intimate reflections of identity. They signal our orientation toward time, trust, risk, and meaning. And when viewed through a philosophical lens, they reveal far more than our financial aspirations—they disclose who we are becoming.

We live in a culture where investing is increasingly automated. Robo-advisors promise optimal allocation with minimal intervention. Index funds invite passive ownership of thousands of companies with a single click. The language of efficiency—of beta, tracking error, Sharpe ratios—dominates the discourse. But in the name of optimisation, something vital is lost: intentionality. *To invest without reflection is to outsource your values to algorithms.* And while automation has its place, an unexamined portfolio often becomes a quiet vessel for unexamined beliefs.

Consider two investors. One builds a portfolio heavily concentrated in green infrastructure, community housing initiatives, and regenerative agriculture. The other holds a basket of fossil fuel producers, defence contractors, and companies known for labour exploitation. Both portfolios may generate returns. But they are not neutral vehicles. They are stories told in capital—stories about what matters, what is tolerated, and what is avoided. *Every asset owned is a tacit endorsement; every omission a decision not to participate.*

This is not an argument for moral purity in investing—such a state is neither attainable nor useful. Rather, it is a call for coherence. A coherent portfolio is not one that never contradicts itself, but one that aligns, over time, with the investor's evolving sense of purpose. Coherence requires not only knowledge of markets, but knowledge of self. What risks feel worthwhile? What industries or instruments feel discordant, no matter the upside? What does it mean to win, financially—and at what cost?

Philosophers have long distinguished between instrumental value and intrinsic value. The former is pursued for what it enables; the latter is pursued for its own sake. Most portfolios are constructed with instrumental goals in mind: security, freedom, status, legacy. But at advanced levels of wealth and reflection, another dimension emerges. Some assets begin to feel intrinsically valuable—not merely as means, but as ends. These may include works of art that evoke awe, parcels of land that evoke memory, or ventures that express belief in a better future. In these cases, the portfolio becomes more than a container of financial utility. It becomes *an artefact of meaning.*

That transition—from tool to artefact—marks a shift in identity. The investor becomes less a consumer of capital and more a curator of consequence. This transition does not happen automatically with age or wealth. It happens through attention. The investor must be willing to ask uncomfortable questions: Why do I hold this asset? What does it imply about what I believe? Am I using money to reinforce who I am, or to escape from deciding?

This is particularly urgent in an era of ambient investing. Financial platforms blur the lines between entertainment, speculation, and planning. Trends arrive and exit with algorithmic velocity. The temptation to mimic is everywhere. One's portfolio can easily become a reaction to noise rather than an expression of signal. But *the investor who mirrors the market loses the ability to see themselves in their portfolio.* True self-knowledge cannot be found in tracking the S&P.

And yet the solution is not isolationism. Coherence does not require shunning mainstream markets or chasing idiosyncrasy for its own sake. It requires something subtler: critical discernment. A portfolio can hold public equities, private ventures, tangible assets, and digital artefacts—but the logic of their inclusion must be intelligible to the investor. That logic need not be shared by others, but it must be felt internally. Without it, the portfolio becomes a hall of mirrors, reflecting nothing but market momentum.

Some of the most thoughtful investors treat their portfolios not as vehicles, but as *vocabularies.* Each position is a word in an unfolding language, expressing beliefs about time, value, trust, and change. Seen this way, investing becomes not just financial strategy but philosophical practice. What you own becomes a way of speaking—to yourself and to the world—about what matters most. In this light, a portfolio is not an endpoint. It is an argument in progress.

Of course, this view requires humility. It is easier to speak of alpha than of alignment. Easier to debate models than to interrogate meaning. But those who avoid such inquiry often find themselves with portfolios that produce wealth but not wisdom. Their financial lives grow in size but not in clarity. And eventually, dissonance sets in. The question then is not "What do I own?" but "What am I complicit in?"

It is here that the investor's internal compass becomes indispensable. Metrics can guide tactics, but only reflection can guide philosophy. This does not mean rejecting performance. Returns matter. But *returns devoid of resonance are hollow.* A brilliant investor once remarked that "money is a terrible master, but a powerful servant." The challenge is not just to accumulate, but to orient—to ensure that the capital you deploy reflects the person you intend to be.

There is also a temporal dimension to this. Portfolios change, as do the people who build them. What made sense five years ago may no longer feel true today. That is not failure; it is growth. A living portfolio should evolve as its architect matures. The willingness to revise one's allocations is not a sign of weakness but of integrity. *Conviction is not rigidity—it is commitment tempered by curiosity.*

And so we return to the idea of the portfolio as mirror. It reflects not only your financial literacy but your ethical priorities, aesthetic sensibilities, psychological tolerances, and temporal perspectives. It shows whether you are building toward permanence or chasing novelty, whether you are hedging against fear or acting from belief. It shows whether you are investing to signal status or to fund substance. It reveals whether you are shaping capital—or being shaped by it.

In the end, every investor leaves behind more than spreadsheets. They leave behind traces of judgement—assets chosen, risks accepted, values expressed. A well-built portfolio is a kind of autobiography in numbers. Not a perfect one, but a telling one. To treat it as such is not to romanticise finance, but to humanise it. Because wealth, at its most refined, is not about domination or escape. It is about alignment—between what we earn, what we own, and who we are becoming.

From Assets to Artifacts: How Investments Become Meaning

Most investment guides focus on yield curves, valuations, and optimised returns. Few pause to ask: what becomes of an asset once it's passed down, displayed, worn, used, or revered? Some investments evolve beyond their monetary role. They become infused with story, sentiment, and meaning. They shift from asset to *artifact*—not in the archaeological sense, but as living, intentional objects of significance. Understanding this transformation is not just a personal exercise in meaning-making. It is a strategic reframe of what it means to own, hold, and build wealth across generations.

Consider a 1960 Château Latour Bordeaux. At auction, it might fetch thousands of pounds. To an oenophile, its value may lie in its terroir, tannin structure, or scarcity. But in the hands of a father who saved it for his daughter's graduation, it becomes more than wine. It becomes a timeline, a commitment, a memory sealed under cork. The market sees a bottle. The family sees a chapter. This is the shift from asset to artifact—and the emotional dividend it pays can compound far beyond what spreadsheets predict.

This phenomenon is neither limited to sentimental families nor idiosyncratic collectors. Increasingly, sophisticated investors are recognising that meaning itself can become a form of durability. Objects that reflect identity, lineage, or legacy tend to outlast speculative cycles. They are less likely to be liquidated during downturns and more likely to be curated with care. When managed with intention, these assets can serve as financial anchors *and* cultural touchstones. They operate on dual registers: one of capital, and one of narrative.

Luxury watch collectors offer a case study. While many purchase watches for resale or appreciation, the most enduring collections are those formed over time, tied to milestones—marriages, births, retirements. A Patek Philippe, famously, is not something you own. It's something you look after for the next generation. That slogan, while commercial in origin, resonates because it speaks to a deep human truth: *we want our choices to mean something after we're gone*. When an asset aligns with memory, values, and aesthetic coherence, it begins to resist mere transactional logic. It matures into an artifact.

This does not imply that one should conflate sentimentality with sound investment. On the contrary, the most meaningful heirloom assets tend to be those that combine aesthetic, emotional, and economic value. A family-owned vineyard. A restored mechanical typewriter used by a bestselling author. A hand-bound first edition passed down through three generations. Each carries a story—and a market value. The key is intentionality. Not every purchase needs to become an artifact. But the investor who never contemplates this dimension may miss a category of value that cannot be digitised or duplicated.

It is also worth asking why this shift matters *now*. In an age of digital ubiquity, meaning has become rare. Algorithmic feeds flatten taste, mass production dulls provenance, and the average object arrives divorced from context. In such an environment, choosing to invest in assets with story—items with craftsmanship, age, and human intentionality—becomes a countercultural act. It is a rejection of the disposable in favour of the durable. And in economic terms, it may be a prescient hedge. As intangible assets proliferate, the scarcity of the meaningful physical grows.

Art is perhaps the most obvious domain where this plays out. While speculative markets abound in the art world, true collectors are driven by something more enduring: connoisseurship, cultural fluency, and often, a desire to steward a vision. The Rothschilds didn't buy paintings merely for price appreciation. They collected to express identity, allegiance, and philosophy. Today, private collections curated over decades are being institutionalised—donated to museums, converted into foundations, or retained as family legacies. These artifacts may not always outperform index funds. But they do something else: *they reflect who we were willing to become.*

This concept is increasingly relevant in alternative asset classes like fine instruments, vintage cars, and rare books. These categories thrive on story. A cello once played in a wartime orchestra. A Porsche raced at Le Mans. A signed letter from Woolf or Baldwin. The financial upside matters, but meaning gives these assets staying power. They are less vulnerable to fads, more insulated from algorithmic churn, and often more deeply integrated into their owners' lives. As a result, they become harder to part with—and therefore, more likely to accrue emotional and cultural weight over time.

There is also a strategic dimension to this. Portfolios that include artifacts can diversify not just by asset class, but by time horizon and intent. While liquid securities can be rebalanced quarterly, heirloom assets operate on generational timelines. Their value lies in continuity, not churn. This encourages a different mindset—less reactive, more reflective. It fosters stewardship over speculation. And as behavioural finance has shown, this shift in posture can itself improve long-term financial outcomes by reducing panic-driven exits and short-termism.

Of course, not every artifact retains its relevance. Cultural tastes shift. What was once treasured may someday be obsolete. But this too is part of the calculus. To curate a portfolio of meaning is to engage in a form of cultural forecasting. What stories, aesthetics, and values will endure? What signals will future generations look for when deciding what to keep? These questions cannot be answered with spreadsheets alone. They require intuition, taste, and philosophical depth—qualities often dismissed in quantitative finance but essential to the long arc of wealth.

One must also grapple with the ethical implications. Who gets to own cultural objects? When does personal legacy intersect with collective heritage? The line between artifact and appropriation can be thin. As investors look toward rare books, indigenous art, or historically significant items, they must do so with sensitivity and rigour. Stewardship implies responsibility, not just possession. Owning something valuable does not automatically entitle one to hoard it. Sometimes, the greatest return comes from sharing—through donation, display, or education.

The most powerful artifacts often transcend the individual. They become communal symbols. The handwritten constitution of a dissolved republic. The diary of a war survivor. The tools of a master craftsman. These are not just collectible items; they are witnesses to history. And in curating them, the modern investor takes on a new role—not just as accumulator of wealth, but as custodian of memory. This is not romanticism. It is strategic humility. It acknowledges that the things we keep may one day speak for us, long after our balance sheets are gone.

Ultimately, the shift from asset to artifact is not about nostalgia. It is about intentionality. It invites the investor to ask: what will this object mean, not just today, but in thirty years? Will it evoke a story worth retelling? Will it embody values worth preserving? Will it still matter when markets move on? These are not just aesthetic questions. They are financial ones—because *meaning compounds*. And in an age obsessed with metrics, that quiet, narrative yield may prove to be the most enduring return of all.

Stewardship, Not Just Strategy – How to Transition from Consumer to Curator, Building a Portfolio That Reflects Values, Not Just Valuations

For most, investing begins with spreadsheets. With yields, charts, forecasts, and benchmarks. But maturity in investing—real depth—rarely ends there. There comes a moment when the sophisticated investor, no longer content with numerical optimisation alone, begins to ask more essential questions: *What does this portfolio say about who I am? What am I enabling with my capital?* And perhaps most revealingly: *Am I accumulating for status, or stewarding for meaning?* These are not rhetorical provocations—they are thresholds. And crossing them marks the difference between treating investments as transactions and understanding them as signals of identity, purpose, and legacy.

Financial markets reward cleverness; but capital, when held thoughtfully, demands conscience. The evolution from consumer to curator is not a rejection of returns—it is a recalibration of what one considers valuable. Curators do not simply acquire—they assemble, protect, and interpret. Their role is not passive; it is interpretive, deliberate, and, above all, enduring. Applying this lens to one's portfolio turns what might otherwise be a mosaic of disconnected positions into a living, breathing collection—a statement of values in motion.

This shift is especially relevant in the context of alternative assets. Unlike publicly traded equities, which often anonymise ownership behind market indices and institutional flows, alternative assets are intimate. They can be touched, seen, and traced. A regenerative farmland parcel is not just a real estate play—it's a vote for sustainable agriculture. A rare whisky cask is not just speculation—it's a trust in time, craft, and continuity. A digital art NFT may be volatile in price, but its ownership may declare allegiance to an aesthetic movement, or the open web. These assets speak, and so does the decision to own them.

The conventional logic of portfolio construction emphasises diversification, liquidity, and performance. But such mechanics, important as they are, offer only a partial account of wealth. They obscure the fact that every investment is also a form of participation. It's participation in a system, a narrative, an economy of belief. When one buys equity in a surveillance-tech company, one doesn't just buy exposure to its earnings—they become complicit in its outcomes. When one invests in local heritage crafts or carbon-offset timberland, they are enlisting their capital in projects that preserve, restore, or challenge. The question, then, becomes not just what the asset will yield—but what it will endorse.

Stewardship as a framework invites investors to see beyond price charts and into the longer arc of consequence. It is not anti-profit. Rather, it is post-naïve. It acknowledges that money never sits still. It flows, ripples, and leverages. And over time, it aligns not just with portfolios, but with character. The curated portfolio, unlike the optimised one, offers not just returns but resonance. Every allocation becomes a reflection, not of market timing, but of intentionality.

Consider the emerging class of impact investors—not just those applying ESG screens, but those actively integrating environmental and social metrics into their mandates. These individuals and institutions are asking: How does this asset improve the world it operates within? How resilient is it to systemic shocks, political tides, or cultural shifts? And most crucially: Do I understand the full footprint—ecological, societal, reputational—of this capital commitment? Their decisions are not slower, but they are deeper. And their success is measured not only in alpha, but in alignment.

Critically, stewardship also introduces a time horizon beyond personal gain. It frames ownership as temporary guardianship. You do not own a vineyard or a historic watch or a family-run business in perpetuity—you care for it during your chapter, and then you pass it on. This changes how risk is evaluated, how relationships are formed, and how liquidity is managed. A curator is not trying to "exit" at the peak, but to transition at the right moment—to the right next steward. This sense of responsibility disciplines decisions in ways that spreadsheets alone cannot.

This model also demands a different form of due diligence. Traditional analysis focuses on cash flow projections, market trends, and comparables. Curatorial diligence adds layers: cultural relevance, ethical provenance, community impact, and symbolic permanence. The question becomes not just, "Can I make money from this?" but "Does it belong in the story I am telling with my capital?" In many cases, this curatorial lens may lead to rejecting investments that others chase—or embracing opportunities others overlook. Either way, it sharpens vision rather than narrowing it.

None of this means abandoning financial rigour. Stewardship, properly understood, is not softness—it is discipline with a conscience. It is knowing not just how to generate returns, but why those returns matter, and to whom. It is balancing the quiet pride of owning something meaningful against the louder temptations of short-term gain. It is resisting the seduction of market cycles and staying rooted in convictions that may not trend on financial media, but endure across generations.

There is also a psychological liberation that comes with this shift. Many investors operate with an undercurrent of unease, chasing returns while privately questioning their real significance. A curator, by contrast, is grounded. They know what they own, why they own it, and what that ownership represents. Their portfolio becomes less a source of anxiety and more a source of articulation. It becomes a form of autobiography—not of consumption, but of contribution.

For those managing generational wealth, the curatorial mindset is especially potent. It provides a framework not only for preserving capital but for transmitting meaning. Heirs may squander riches they did not earn, but they are far less likely to squander stories they understand. A portfolio built with values communicates implicitly: This is who we are. This is what matters. This is how we show up in the world.

As economic volatility intensifies and markets increasingly reward novelty over substance, the need for this framework grows stronger. The antidote to distraction is not more information, but deeper conviction. The antidote to overconsumption is not asceticism, but discernment. And the antidote to hollow investing is not radical activism, but quiet curation.

None of this will appeal to everyone—and it need not. But for the investor who is ready to ask harder questions, who wants their capital to reflect not only intelligence but integrity, stewardship offers both a philosophy and a practice. It is a call to care. To select with purpose. To own with reverence. And to remember that the most enduring returns are often those we cannot measure—but only feel.

This, then, is the quiet revolution of the 21st-century investor—not the conquest of markets, but the curation of meaning. A transition from ownership as accumulation to ownership as authorship. From strategy as dominance to strategy as stewardship. Not just what you hold, but *how you hold it.* And in that distinction lies the real power—and responsibility—of wealth.

A Final Prompt: What Are You Really Buying?

Every investment is a choice—not just about capital allocation, but about belief, attention, and value. In the language of finance, we speak of portfolios, diversification, risk-adjusted returns. But underneath that technical scaffolding lies something more personal, more telling. At its core, an investment reflects what we think will matter tomorrow. It expresses what we trust, what we honour, and what we believe has enduring worth. And in a world saturated with financial noise, fads, and speculative distractions, this act of choosing carries profound meaning.

Modern investing, particularly in alternative assets, demands more than strategy; it demands clarity of intention. A collector of rare books may think of themselves as preserving culture. A buyer of fractional whisky casks might see an echo of tradition and patience in a hyper-accelerated age. Even an NFT investor, amid market volatility, may be signalling an early vote of confidence in how digital authenticity will be defined. These choices are not just economic—they are autobiographical. They tell a story about who we are and where we think the world is heading. The question, then, is not merely what you are buying. It is what you are affirming, endorsing, and inviting into your life through ownership.

This is not a moralistic critique of profit-making. Wealth-building is an essential endeavour, and finance, when practised wisely, can be a force for resilience and freedom. But the challenge—especially in opaque or speculative markets—is to build wealth with awareness, not accident. Too many portfolios reflect borrowed conviction: a splash of crypto because colleagues are talking about it, a slice of art exposure because a celebrity endorsed it, a rushed venture investment dressed up as visionary thinking. When ownership becomes mimicry, we risk accumulating not just bad investments, but distorted identities.

Clarity begins with the discipline of questioning. What does this asset actually represent? What values or assumptions are embedded in it? Who benefits from my holding it—not just financially, but culturally or socially? Is it part of a narrative I want to participate in, or simply a story I've been sold? This mode of inquiry doesn't mean paralysis or excessive scepticism. It simply means reclaiming intention. It's about ensuring that what sits in your portfolio is there because *you chose it*—not because the algorithm or the algorithmically influenced crowd whispered it into your ear.

Consider the distinction between market price and personal value. A vintage wristwatch may not deliver market-beating returns, yet to its owner, it may serve as a bridge across generations, a symbol of craft, a rejection of planned obsolescence. A stake in a regenerative farm may yield modest annual returns, yet resonate with a belief in ecological repair and food sovereignty. Conversely, a trendy digital collectible with unclear provenance may spike in value, but if it fails to align with your sense of permanence, it may feel more like noise than signal. The point is not to elevate sentiment over return, but to recognise that *long-term conviction often emerges from meaning*—not hype.

Even in traditional markets, seasoned investors understand this. Family offices often emphasise legacy. Endowments weigh moral and social impact. Visionary entrepreneurs invest in systems they believe will underpin the future, not just generate alpha. This is not idealism. It's durability. Assets held with clarity, integrity, and personal alignment tend to be understood more deeply, weather volatility with more patience, and earn their place in a portfolio with greater scrutiny. When you know *why* you own something, you are less likely to be shaken by headlines, groupthink, or fear.

The same philosophy applies at the margins of finance, where innovation and risk converge. In alternative asset classes—whisky, timberland, digital tokens, rare sneakers—the line between value and vanity can blur. It's tempting to be drawn to novelty for novelty's sake, or to project status through exotic holdings. But the wiser approach is to ask: does this asset amplify who I am becoming, or simply distract me from uncertainty? Does it signal a thoughtful view of the world, or is it a bet disguised as a belief? These are uncomfortable questions, but they are essential. They inoculate us against fads and reinforce intentionality.

Curation, in this light, becomes more than strategy—it becomes stewardship. You are not merely acquiring things. You are assembling a worldview. Each asset is a tile in a mosaic, a sentence in a story, a reflection of intellectual taste. And like all meaningful collections—whether of books, wines, or relationships—it is not the volume that defines it, but the coherence. A well-curated portfolio, like a well-curated life, reveals something deeper than balance sheets: it reveals character.

There is, of course, a humility required here. No one sees the future with precision. Even the most thoughtful investor will misjudge markets or misread signals. That is not failure—that is the price of participation. But when an investor leads with clarity and intention, the mistakes become teachers, not trauma. They reinforce the value of discernment, the need for context, the importance of continuous learning. In this way, the act of investing becomes an evolving discipline, not just a financial one, but a philosophical and psychological one too.

We live in an age where noise is cheap and signal is scarce. Financial commentary is endless, investment platforms are frictionless, and data flows faster than discernment. Yet amidst this acceleration, the most valuable asset remains perspective. And perspective, unlike price, cannot be outsourced. It must be earned—through reflection, through rigor, and through the willingness to ask uncomfortable questions.

So what are you really buying? Not just in ticker symbols or token IDs, but in time, attention, and identity? What do your holdings whisper about your worldview? What do they affirm about what you believe is durable, beautiful, and necessary? These are not abstract musings. They are the compass points for navigating a world where meaning competes with momentum, and ownership is both a right and a responsibility.

As this book closes, let this final prompt linger—not as a call to perfection, but to presence. Investing, at its best, is not just about growing wealth. It's about growing clarity. The assets you choose are not just bets on markets. They are bets on what you believe is worth keeping.

About the Author

Julian Thorne is a lifelong student of value—how we find it, how we measure it, and why we pass it down. With a background in cultural history and a fascination for the psychology of wealth, Julian writes at the intersection of economics, aesthetics, and personal meaning. His work explores how alternative investments—from whiskey casks to royalty streams—serve as reflections of who we are and what we choose to preserve. Drawing from years of firsthand research, conversations with collectors, and deep dives into fringe markets, Julian's writing invites readers to invest not only with their capital, but with their curiosity. He lives quietly, collects deliberately, and believes the best assets are the ones that outlive us.

www.ingramcontent.com/pod-product-compliance
Lightning Source LLC
Chambersburg PA
CBHW020240250926
51848CB00007BA/427
* 9 7 8 9 3 7 1 7 7 6 8 9 9 *